ARM in Space

Patrick H. Stakem
(c) 2019

Table of Contents

Author...4

Introduction..5

    ARM Cortex..7

        Cortex-A...7

        Cortex-R...10

        Cortex-M..10

        ARM 64 11

ARM Multicore..12

    Cache Coherency in Multicore...............................13

    Raspberry Pi architectures.....................................14

    Arduino Architecture..15

        Media Processing..16

        Graphics Processing 16

    RadHard ARM Cortex-M0......................................22

    SAMRH71...22

    VA10820 22

    High-Performance Spaceflight Computing Program...........23

    Strength in numbers...23

ARM at work..24

        Consumables inventory.......................................25

        Thermal management...25

        Electrical Power/energy management.................25

        Antenna Pointing..26

        Safe Hold mode..26

        Science Data Processing.....................................26

        NASA Data Processing Levels Definition.................27

The Space environment...30

    Zero G issues 30

    Vacuum..31

    Thermal environment 31

    Orbital Debris..32

    Mechanical and Structural Issues...........................32

    ESD sensitivity..32

    Spacecraft Charging..32

Radiation effects...33
Cumulative dose and single events......................35
Rad-Hard Software 36
Watchdog Core..37
Radiation Damage Mitigation.............................38
Open Source versus Proprietary.............................38
ARM Flight software...40
Linux...41
cFE/cFS..41
ARM Application Software..................................47
Data Bases, and Electronic Data Sheets..............47
Beowulf...48
What Space Missions use ARM?.............................49
Mars Helicopter Scout....................................49
Cosmos...50
Afterword...50
Glossary of Terms...51
References...59
Resources...64

Author

Mr. Patrick H. Stakem received a Bachelors degree in Electrical Engineering from Carnegie-Mellon University, and Masters Degrees in Physics and Computer Science from the Johns Hopkins University.

He began his career in Aerospace with Fairchild Industries on the ATS-6 (Applications Technology Satellite-6), program, a communication satellite that developed much of the technology for the TDRSS (Tracking and Data Relay Satellite System). At Fairchild, Mr. Stakem made the amazing discovery that computers were put onboard the spacecraft. He quickly made himself the expert on their support. He followed the ATS-6 Program through its operation phase, and worked on other projects at NASA's Goddard Space Flight Center including the Hubble Space Telescope, the International Ultraviolet Explorer (IUE), the Solar Maximum Mission (SMM), some of the Landsat missions, and others. He was posted to NASA's Jet Propulsion Laboratory for the MARS-Jupiter-Saturn (MJS-77), which later became the Voyager mission, which is still operating and returning data from outside the solar system at this writing. He has received NASA's Space Shuttle Program Managers commendation award.

Mr. Stakem is affiliated with the Whiting School of Engineering of the Johns Hopkins University. He has direct hands-on experience with the ARM family, linux, and Beowulf.

By 2010, over 6 billion ARM chips had been sold, mostly into the smartphone market. ARM is the target architecture for the GNU/linux-based Android operating system, and the ARM has ports of OpenSolaris, FreeBSD, OpenBSD, NetBSD, various GNU/linux variations, including Gentoo, Debian, Slackware, and Ubuntu, and Windows Embedded.

Introduction

The ARM processor has come a long way from an obscure British microprocessor of the 1980's to being the dominant basis for the current generation of smart phones, and tablet computers, as well as its use in space They are also in television set-top boxes, routers, and embedded applications. The ARM architecture units represent the highest volume of 32-bit processors being shipped, as of this writing.

The ARM started out on the desktop, but along the way, got diverted mostly to embedded use. Now, more powerful ARM chips are challenging the pc and server markets.

ARM is the baseline for small computers and embedded controllers such as the RaspberryPi and the Arduino series. These are provided as licensable products by ARM Holdings Ltd. ARM Holdings is owned by Softbank Group's Vision Fund. Softbank is a Japanese multinational holding company. ARM Holdings does not produce chips. The Intellectual Property (IP) of the ARM is a proprietary, license-able product of ARM Holdings. Numerous company's produce a wide variety of ARM chips, under the license.

ARM's can be found on space missions, most likely in Cubesats, but also on the ISS. At the moment there are several models of a rad-hard Arduino-class microcontroller, and an ongoing NASA-USAF project to produce a radiation hard version of an Arm, a number cruncher capable of hosting an operating system.

One of the big problems in space electronics is the environment, particularly that of radiation. There are various mitigation's, and ARM's have flow on satellite missions, some of which are discussed here

The Surrey Satellite Technology Nanosat Applications Platform

(SNAP-1) was launched on June 28, 2000. The onboard computer (OBC) was based on Intel's StrongArm SA-1100 with 4 Mbytes of 32-bit wide EDAC protected SRAM. The error correction logic could correct 2 bits in every 8 using a modified Hamming code and the errors were "washed" from memory by software to prevent accumulation from multiple single-event upsets. There was 2 Mbytes of Flash memory containing a simple bootloader which loaded the application software into SRAM.

The NanoMind A712D is an onboard computer for Cubesats. It uses as 32-bit ARM cpu, with 2 megabytes of RAM, and 8 megabytes of flash memory. It can also support a MicroSD flash card. It has a Can bus and a I^2C interface. It comes with an extensive software library and real time operating system. Special applications, such as attitude determination and control code are available. It is tolerant to temperatures from -40 to 85 degrees C, but is not completely rad-hard.

The CFC-300 from InnoFlight Inc. of San Diego is another example. It uses the Xilinx Zynq System-on-a-chip architecture. That provides both FPGA capability, and an Arm Cortex A-9 dual core cpu. It has 256 Megabytes of SDRAM, and 32 megabytes of flash. There are multiple synchronous serial interfaces. Daughter cards provide support for SpaceWire, Ethernet, RapidIO, RS-422, and thermistor inputs and heater drive outputs. It can be used with linux or VxWorks.

The Intrepid Cubesat OBC from Tyvak Uses a 400 MHz Atmel processor, and has 128 Mbytes of SDRAM, and 512 Mbytes of flash memory. It draws between 200-300 milliwatts. It includes a command and data handling system, and an onboard electrical power controller. It supports ethernet, RS-232, USB, and the SPI and I^2C interfaces. It includes a JTAG debugging interface. Similar to the Arduino, it supports 3-axis gyros, a 3-axis magnetometer, accelerometers, and a variety of i^2c-interfaced sensors. The Microcontroller is an ARM architecture, with digital signal processing extensions. It has a built-in Image Sensor interface.

There are now several Arduino-class microcontrollers available in rad-hard versions, and one ARM Raspberry-Pi like product being developed by Boeing for NASA and the Air Force with delivery in 2021.

ARM Cortex

We will briefly discuss the ARM architecture families. The ARM Cortex processors are the latest in the 32-bit series, and extend into multicore and 64-bit models for higher performance. There are three basic models of the Cortex processors, targeting different applications areas. These are the Cortex-A, Cortex-M, and Cortex-R. The Cortex models began to appear in 2004.

Cortex-A

Cortex-A processors are targeted to the smartphone and mobile computing markets, as well as digital television, set-top boxes, and printers. They include a memory management unit, a prerequisite to supporting modern operating systems.

The Cortex-A5 optionally supports floating point and NEON media processing. The memory management was improved, and virtual memory is supported. The design is targeted to energy efficiency. Voltages are 1.0 or 1.1 volts, with clock speeds to 1 GHz. Up to 4 cores are supported. Instruction and data L1 caches can extend to 64k each.

NEON implements an advanced SIMD instruction set and was first introduced with the ARM Cortex –A8 model. This is an extension of the FPU with a quad Multiply-and-Accumulate (MAC) unit and additional 64-bit and 128-bit registers.

Single instruction, multiple data (SIMD) describes computers with multiple processing elements that perform the same operation on multiple data simultaneously. Thus, such machines exploit data level parallelism. Vector processing is where a single operation is applied to all elements of an array of data.

The Cortex-A8 is a superscalar architecture, with dual instruction issue. The NEON SIMD unit is optional, as is floating point support. The architecture supports Thumb-2 and Jazelle, but only single core. Advanced branch prediction algorithms provide an accuracy rate reportedly approaching 95%. Up to a four megabyte Level-2 cache is provided. There is a 128-bit SIMD engine. Cortex A-8 chips have been implemented by Samsung, TI, and Freescale, among others.

The Cortex-A9 can have multiple cores that are multi-issue superscalar and support out-of-order and speculative execution using register renaming. It uses an 8-stage pipeline. Two instructions per cycle can be decoded. There are up to 64k of 4-way set associative Level-1 cache, with up to 512k of Level 2. A 64-bit Harvard architecture memory access allows for maximum bandwidth. Four doubleword writes take five machine cycles. Floating point units and a media processing engine are available for each core. The Cortex-A supports the Thumb-2 instructions, which are 16-bit subsets of ARM instructions.

The Cortex-A9 is implemented in a series of system-on-a-chip devices from multiple manufacturers. As an example, the STMElectronics SPEAr1310 is a dual-core Cortex-A SMP. It has dual cores, and can support either symmetric or asymmetric multiprocessing. It has a 32k instruction and a 32k data cache at Level 1. The Level 2 cache is unified, and is 512k bytes in size. The on-chip inter-processor bus is 64 bits wide. The chip includes 32k of bootrom and 32k of SRAM, with support for external NAND or NOR flash and static ram.

The Cortex chip includes dual Gigabit ports, three fast Ethernet, three PCIe links, three SATA ports, dual USB-2, dual CAN bus, dual HDLC controllers, dual I²C ports, and six UARTs operating up to 5 Megabaud. There is an integrated LCD controller with touchscreen support, a keyboard controller, and a memory card interface. It supports thirteen timers and a real time clock, in addition to a cryptographic accelerator. Included are dual 8-channel DMA controllers, a JPEG codec in hardware, and 8-input, 10-bit A/D, and JTAG support.

The Cortex-A15 is multicore, and has an out-of-order superscalar pipeline. The chip was introduced in 2012, and is available from TI, NVidia, Samsung, and others. It can address a terabyte of memory. The integer pipeline is 15 stages long, and the floating point pipeline is up to 25 stages. The instruction issue is speculative. There can be 4 cores per cluster, two clusters per chip. Each core has separate 32k data and instruction caches. The level-2 cache controller supports up to 4 megabytes per cluster. DSP and NEON SIMD are supported, as is floating point. Hardware virtualization support is included. Both Thumb-2 and Jazelle modes are included.

Hardware assisted virtualization is an example of platform virtualization. It uses assistance from the hardware to provide full virtualization, so unmodified guest operating systems can be supported. The technique was first used on IBM System/370 mainframe machines in 1972.

Virtualization is done with a second stage of address translation with its own page tables. I/O can be virtualized. The Hypervisor runs in a new privilege mode, unique to it. The mode is entered with a Hypervisor Call. The Virtualization privilege mode is a new third privilege level. There is the user code level, the operating system level, the Hypervisor level, and a TrustZone Privilege level, at the top. The Embedded Xen product also supports virtualization on the ARM architecture.

In the ARM, before virtualization, the Operating System controlled the memory resource. There is now a second level of address translation. Where virtual addresses used to map to physical addresses, they now map to Intermediate addresses, which are then mapped to physical addresses by the Hypervisor.

Interrupts are another issue. An interrupt might need to go to the current or another guest operating system, the Hypervisor, or an operating system in the TrustZone. Physical interrupts go to the Hypervisor first; if they need to go to a guest operating system, this is handled by a "virtual" interrupt.

Since the ARM architecture uses memory-mapped I/O, that process is also virtualized. Virtual devices are created by emulation.

Cortex-R

The ARM Cortex-R product addresses hard real-time, safety critical applications. It has specific features to address performance in real-time applications. These include an instruction cache and a data cache, a floating point coprocessor, and an extended 8-stage pipeline. Cortex-R supports the Thumb and Thumb-2 instructions as well as ARM. Up to 64-bit data structures are supported. The compiler must be aware of which architecture is used as the code target, to introduce the proper optimizations for the various models. As with different implementations of the ISA-32 instruction set from Intel, different implementation architectures require different optimization strategies. The correct optimization for one chip could be the worst-case approach for a different implementation. Cortex-R addresses applications in robotics and avionics/space applications.

Cortex-M

The Cortex M models are microcontrollers. There are four models, the Cortex-M0, 1, 2, and 3. All are binary compatible. The M0 and M1 are based on the ARMv6, the M3 is based on the ARMv7, and the M4 is based on the ARM-V7-ME. The Thumb and Thumb-2 subsets are supported. The M3 model has a single cycle 32x32 hardware multiply and 10-12 cycle hardware divide instruction. The M4 adds Digital Signal Processing instructions such as a single-cycle 16/32 bit multiply-accumulate, and supports full Thumb and Thumb-2 instruction set. The IEEE-754 floating point unit is included with the M4. A nested, vectored interrupt controller is included. The 256 interrupts are fully deterministic, and an NMI is included. Cortex-M does not support the instruction and data caches, or the coprocessor interface, and has only a 3-stage pipeline. Only the M3 and M4 models support the Memory Protection Unit. The M3 instruction set provides a pair of synchronization primitives for a guaranteed atomic read-modify-write operation, which is critical to real-time operating systems.

Examples of the chip include the Atmel SAM3 series and the TI Stellaris models. These include flash and sram, timers including a real-time clock and watchdog, PWM for motor control, Ethernet, CAN, USB, and UART functions, and A/D's. The M4 models are made by Atmel, Freescale, STMicroelectronics, and TI.

The SAM RH71 microcontroller product from Microchip uses a Cortex M7 architecture. This unit is particularly power efficient. It has a six stage superscalar pipeline and implements branch prediction. Floating point can also be supported. Internal buses are 64-bits wide.

The VA10820 microcontroller uses the Cortex M0, as does the PA32KAS and Protec products. These are available as rad-hard parts. The Mo is optimized for small size. They have a 3-stage pipeline, and are 32-bits. There is hardware multiply, but no floating point unit.

ARM 64

ARM architecture version 8 (ARMv8) defines support for 64-bit data and addressing, and multicore operations. It is dual-issue superscalar, so almost twice as many instructions per clock can be executed. All instructions are 32-bits, allowing for more rapid decode. There are 31 general purpose registers. It can include the NEON SIMD instruction set extension, and a vector floating point unit. It supports the Jazelle architecture. Branches are optimized with an advanced branch predictor that can achieve success rates approaching 95%. The virtual address space is 48 bits, with a 40-bit physical address space supported initially. The ARM v8 ISA allows for operation in 32-bit and 64-bit modes. It includes virtualization support, NEON SIMD support, and enhanced security, while maintaining compatibility with ARMv7.

The Version 8 is implemented by Freescale Semiconductor, Samsung, TI, and others. This architecture will supplement the ARM architectures dominance in smart phones, tablets, and embedded systems, with competition in top-end desktop and server applications.

Embedded refers to special purpose computers that are a part of a larger system, as opposed to generic desktop computers, tablets, and servers. Embedded systems are for specific purposes; they are not necessarily general purpose. They may have a limited or no human interface, but usually support complex I/O. The embedded computer can be characterized by the parameters of its central processing unit, memory, and input/output (I/O). The CPU parameters of importance are speed, power consumption, and price. The memory parameters include power consumption, speed, volatility, and size or capacity. I/O characteristics must be matched to external systems components, and there are many options.

ARM Multicore

The latest ARM architecture supports multicore (currently, up to 8-core) architectures. Both symmetrical and asymmetrical implementations are included. Putting a lot of cores on a single substrate is challenging, but getting them to work together co-cooperatively and non-intrusively is difficult. The CoreLink cache coherent interconnect system IP, for use in multicore applications, is one emerging solution. Some problems are inherently parallelizable, but most are not. Not many problem domains scale linearly with the amount of computing horsepower available. Such embarrassingly parallel applications are rarely of practical interest.

The Cortex-A9 microarchitecture comes with either a scalable multicore processor, the Cortex-A9 MPCore™ or as a more traditional processor, the Cortex-A9 single core processor. The configuration includes 16, 32, or 64KB four-way associative L1 caches, with up to 8MB of L2 cache through the optional L2 cache controller. The memory architecture of the A9 is Harvard, with separate code and data paths. It can sustain four double-word write transfers every 5 cycles. It includes a high efficiency superscalar pipeline, which removes dependencies between adjacent instructions. It has double the floating point performance of previous units. Up to a 2 GHz clock is currently feasible. Two instructions per cycle are decoded. Instruction execution is speculative, using dynamic register renaming. A similar technique is used to unroll loops in the hardware at execution time. There are four execution pipelines fed from the issue queue, and out-of-order dispatch is supported, as is out-of-order write-back. Items can be marked as non-cachable, write back, or write through.

Cache Coherency in Multicore

In multicore architectures, each CPU core may have its own L1 cache, but share L2 caches with other cores. Local data in the L1 caches must be consistent with data in other L1 caches. If one core changes a value in cache due to a write operation, that data needs to be changed in other caches as well (if they hold the same item).

This problem is well known and studies from the field of multiprocessing. The issues can be addressed by several mechanisms. In cache snooping, each cache monitors the others for

13

changes. If a change in value is seen, the local cached copy is invalidated. This means it will have to be re-accessed from the next level before use. A global directory of cached data can also be maintained. Several protocols for cache coherency include MSI, MESI, and others.

Raspberry Pi architectures

The Raspberry Pi is a small, inexpensive, single board computer based on the ARM architecture. It is targeted to the academic market. It originally used the Broadcom BCM2835 system-on-a-chip, which has a 700 MHz ARM processor, a video GPU, and currently 512 M of RAM. It uses an SD card for storage. The Raspberry Pi runs the GNU/linux and FreeBSD operating systems. It was first sold in February 2012. Sales reached ½ million units by the Fall. Due to the open source nature of the software, Raspberry Pi applications and drivers can be downloaded from various sites. It requires a single power supply, and dissipates a few watts. It has USB ports, and an Ethernet controller. It does not have a real-time clock, but one can easily be added. It outputs video in HDMI resolution, and supports audio output. I/O includes 8 general purpose I/O lines, UART, I2C bus, and SPI bus. The Raspberry Pi comes in 32-bit or 64-bit variants.

The Raspberry Pi design comes from the Raspberry Pi Foundation in the UK, which was formed to promote the study of Computer Science. The Raspberry Pi is seen as the successor to the original BBC Microcomputer by Acorn, which resulted in the ARM processor.

The Raspberry Pi can be used a a desktop/tablet computer for general purpose applications. The B+ version of the Pi has a Image System Pipeline (ISP) to directly handle data from a digital camera, and can be programmed with OpenGL. This is a GPU with 20 processing stages. It can handle a frame rate of 30 images per second, with 1080 pixel resolution. It uses 16-way vector code, and the pipeline operates at 250 Mhz.

14

Arduino Architecture

The Arduino is an open source design for a Microcontroller. There's a large variety to choose from, from simple 8-bit to 32-bit . As a microcontroller, the Arduinos are targeted to sensing and control, often real-time operations. They are not heavy duty number crunchers. They have a wide variety of I/O interfaces. If they run an operating system, it would usually be real-time. They can also just run dedicated code, without a distinct operating system. A boot loader is included.

Lacking some operating system support such as memory mapping, Arduinos are generally run without one. The code handles those operating systems functions as necessary, such as the interrupt vector setup at Power-up. Expansion modules, called shields, plug directly into the Arduino motherboard.

Inherently simpler than the Raspberry Pi, Rad-Hard Arduino-class microcontrollers are currently available.

Media Processing

Media Processing refers to operations on audio and video data structures. These are Digital Signal Processing operations. Image compression and decompression operations on streaming video in real time is an example. They can provide advanced onboard processing of sensor data, and do tasks such as pattern extraction.

The ARM NEON is a general purpose SIMD engine operating on multimedia data structures. It has a 128-bit architecture, and serves as an extension for the ARM Cortex-A. It has sixteen 128-bit registers.

The Advanced SIMD extension, marketed as NEON technology, is a combined 64- and 128-bit SIMD instruction set that provides standardized acceleration for media and signal processing applications. NEON can execute MP3 audio decoding on CPUs running at 10 MHz and can run the GSM AMR (Adaptive Multi-Rate) speech codec at no more than 13 MHz. It features a comprehensive instruction set, separate register files and independent execution hardware. NEON supports 8-, 16-, 32- and 64-bit integer and single-precision (32-bit) floating-point data and operates in SIMD operations for handling audio and video processing as well as graphics and gaming processing. In NEON, the SIMD supports up to 16 operations at the same time. The NEON hardware shares the same floating-point registers as used in VFP.

Graphics Processing

The ARM Multimedia processors are graphics processing units. They do graphics operations on graphics configured data. In the same sense that regular CPU's operate on integers and boolean data, dedicated floating point units operate on floating point data, and GPU's operate on graphics data.

A GPU can also operate on integer and floating point data, but has been optimized to address graphics data, and its operations.

Graphics data can be integer or floating point. Generally, it is organized in 1 dimensional arrays (vectors) or multi-dimensional arrays. Since we will see later that we can under use our GPU to do general purpose processing, there is nothing special about the data format. Keep in mind, the GPU does not implement logic functions.

To use the GPU in a general purpose role, we basically have to reformulate our computational problem in terms of the graphics operations the GPU provides. The OpenCL language, widely used in GPU programming, is general purpose.

A GPU is a specialized computer architecture intended to manipulate image data at high rates. The GPU devices are highly parallel, and specifically designed to handle image data, and operations on that data. They do this much faster than a programmed general purpose CPU. Most desktop machines have the GPU function on a video card or integrated with their CPU. Originally, GPU's were circuit card based. Now, they're chips, and increasingly, multicore chips. GPU operations are very memory intensive. The GPU design is customized to SIMD type operations.

The instruction set of the GPU is specific to graphics operations on block data. The requirements were driven by the demands of 2-D and 3-D video games on pc's, phones, tablets, and dedicated gaming units. As GPU units became faster and more capable, they began to consume more power (and thus generate more heat) than the associated CPU's. The GPU operations are typically memory intensive, so fast access to memory is critical.

A GPU is generally a dataflow architecture, as opposed to a control-flow, Von Neumann machine. The instructions executed depend on the inputs, to the extent that the order of execution is nondeterministic. On general purpose machines implementing graphics processing code, the behavior would be deterministic.

Although designed to process video data, some GPU's have been used as adjunct data processors and accelerators in other areas involving vectors and matrices, with operations such as the inverse discrete cosine transform. Types of higher-level processing implemented by GPU's include texture mapping, polygon rendering, object rotation, and coordination system transformation. They also support object shading operations, data oversampling, and interpolation. GPU's find a major application area in video decoding. GPU's can be used to accelerate database operations such as gather and scatter, vertex operations. In space, these would operate on sensed data.

GPU's can tackle the embarrassingly parallel problems in engineering and physics, those that map to multiple parallel tasks that can be executed simultaneously. Examples of some of these applications include protein folding and ray tracing.

You can do general purpose computing on a GPU, although it may not be the ideal platform. It requires you to recast your computation in a way the GPU understands, which is to say, in terms of graphics. So, we might have to represent the data as a 2D or 3D object, that we can apply the GPU's operations on. GPU's are special purpose devices that have instruction sets that are not general purpose, and are intended specifically for graphics data processing, and problems that lend themselves to stream or vector processing. GPU's are stream processors, in that they operate in parallel on multiple data. Given the right problem, that is map-able into the GPU's architecture, a huge performance gain of orders of magnitude can be achieved, over regular CPU's.

One figure of merit in GPU's is their *arithmetic intensity*, defined as the number of operations per memory access. You might think of this as a computation:communication ratio.

GPU's are used for coordinate system transformations, and for science data processing. The GPU can implement such operations as shading, codec, mapping, video decoding, and 3D image manipulation.

Extensive code libraries exist for GPU's, and different problem domains, from physics modeling, to video gaming and virtual reality. API's include OpenGL and Directx. OpenGL, the Open (source) graphics libraries operate across languages and platforms. It was introduced in 1992. It is an industry standard, and claims scalability from hand-held to supercomputer. It consists of a series of library functions, callable from most computer languages. DirectX, similarly, has a set of runtime libraries. It is a Microsoft product. There are other libraries of graphics functions available as well.

GPU's need high bandwidth connections to data. They are beginning to include fast, hardware managed, multi-level caches. The architectures differ from that of general purpose caches, since the GPU is mostly accessing vector data, from consecutive memory locations. GPU's have large register files on chip to reduce access time to frequently used data.

The instruction set of the GPU is specific to graphics operations on block data. The requirements were driven by the demands of 2-D and 3-D data. As GPU units became faster and more capable, they consume more power (and thus generate more heat) than the associated CPU's.

Single instruction, multiple data (SIMD) describes computers with multiple processing elements that perform the same operation on multiple data simultaneously. Thus, such machines exploit data level parallelism. Vector processing is where a single operation is applied to an entire 1-dimensional array of data.

The Cortex-A15 is multi-core, and has an out-of-order superscalar pipeline. The chip was introduced in 2012, and is available from TI, NVidia, Samsung, and others. It can address a terabyte of memory. The integer pipeline is 15 stages long, and the floating point pipeline is up to 25 stages. The instruction issue is speculative. There can be 4 cores per cluster, two clusters per chip. Each core has separate 32k data and instruction caches. The level-2 cache controller supports up to 4 megabytes per cluster. DSP and NEON SIMD are supported, as is floating point. Hardware virtualization support is included.

Rad hard Arm

There are several Rad-Hard ARM microcontrollers available at this writing. There use either the M7 or M0 architecture. These are equivalent to the Arduino architectures in common use as microcontrollers.

In 2016, NASA and the Air Force Research Labs approached industry about a new, rad-hard ARM processor. This was termed the High Performance Spacecraft Computing chip. Boeing won the competitive contract to provide the units, with the University of Southern California providing the software., which is required to be Open Source. It is based on the ARM A53 (64 bit) architecture, manufactured in a rad-hard-by-design cell libraries. The A53 includes the NEON single instruction multiple data (simd) processor. In various architectural trade study's, a rad-hard, general purpose multicore was the chosen architecture. This will be produced by a rad-hard-by design methodology, and incorporates Serial RapidIO. The Program is managed by the Jet Propulsion Lab.

The Processor architecture is called a chiplet, and contains an ARM, 64-bit, 8 core cpu. Each chiplet can have 3 levels of cache, SRAM, DRAM, and MRAM. The computer assembly supports ethernet and spacewire. There is also dual PCVIe busses, and high speed serial I/O Delivery is due by April of 2021.

A Rad-Hard ARM Cortex-M0 is a microcontroller from Protec GmbH, a company with 30 years experience in rad-hard electronics, and a portfolio of processor and support parts. It provides a Cortex M0 cpu, operating at 50 Mhz, and using 3.3 volts. Memory includes 16k each of data and program memory. Error detection and correction is included. It can interface with up to 36 megabytes of external memory. It includes GPIO pins, that can also be used as interrupts. There are 32 general purpose counter-timers, and dual UARTS. There are dual SPI interfaces.

All internal registers are triple-modular redundant. It is hardened to a TID of 300 krad, and is latch-up immune to 100 MeV-cm^2/mg. It comes in a 1.3 x 1.3 inch, 188 pin package. Not a computational powerhouse, it is a capable controller.

The SAMRH71 is a rad-hard-by-design microcontroller chip from Microchip, based on their commercial grade SAMv71. It is a 32-bit Cortex M7. The rad hard version includes Spacewire and MIL-STD-1553 I/O. The radiation performance is a LET of 62 MeV/CM^2 with an SEU greater than 20 and a TID of 100 Krad. This microcontroller operates up to 100 MHz. Besides the rad-hard part, a less-expensive radiation-tolerant part is also available. The part includes CAN and Ethernet interfaces.

Vorago Technologies is marketing the VA10820, an ARM Cortex-M0 that is hard to 300krad. It operates at 50 MHz, and includes JTAG. It has 32k of data memory, and 128k of program memory. Memory EDAC and scrub are included. It is a microcontroller, with 54 GPIO's, dual i2c, dual UART, and triple SPI's. It has a remarkable 24 32-bit counter-timers, and includes PWM's, and a watchdog timer. All internal registers are TMR.

The Atmega S-128 is a rad-hard microcontroller, with the Cortex M7 architecture. It has Spacewire and 1553 bus. It can work up to a total integrated dose of 100 Krad.

RadHard ARM Cortex-M0

This unit is a microcontroller from Protec GmbH, a company with 30 years experience in rad-hard electronics, and a portfolio of processor and support parts. It provides a Cortex M0 cpu, operating at 50 Mhz, and using 3.3 volts. Memory includes 16k each of data and program memory. Error detection and correction is included. It can interface with up to 36 megabytes of external memory. It includes GPIO pins, that can also be used as interrupts. There are 32 general purpose counter-timers, and dual UARTS. There are dual SPI interfaces.

All internal registers are triple-modular redundant. It is hardened to a TID of 300 krad, and is latch-up immune to 100 MeV-cm^2/mg. It comes in a 1.3 x 1.3 inch, 188 pin package. Not a computational powerhouse, it is a capable controller.

SAMRH71

The SAMRH71 is a rad-hard-by-design microcontroller chip from Microchip, based on their commercial grade SAMv71. It is a 32-bit Cortex M7. The rad hard version includes Spacewire and MIL-STD-1553 I/O. The radiation performance is a LET of 62 MeV/CM^2 with an SEU greater than 20 and a TID of 100 Krad. This microcontroller operates up to 100 MHz. Besides the rad-hard part, a less-expensive radiation-tolerant part is also available. The part includes CAN and Ethernet interfaces.

VA10820

This chip, from Vorago, is based on the Cortex M0 architecture. It is 32 bits, rated beyond 300 krad, and is latch-up immune to 110

MeV-cm^2/mg. It includes 32k of data, and 128 k of program memory. For I/O, it includes dual UART's, dual I^{2}C's, and three SPI's. It comes in a 128 pin ceramic package. The memory, using EDAC, is rated at fewer than 10^{-13} errors/bit-day. It implements EDAC, and TMR on critical functions. The similar PA32KAS offers 16k data and program data

High-Performance Spaceflight Computing Program

Looming on the horizon is a product from the ongoing AFSL/NASA Next Generation Space Processor (NGSP) Project. This will not be a rad-hard Arm-based microcontroller, but rather something similar to the Raspberry Pi architecture. It will have a 64-bit product, with 8 cores. It will be a capable number cruncher, and will support common open-source software, both operating systems and high-end applications. It is based on the ARM Cortex A53 architecture. This unit is superscalar, with dual units. It has an 8-stage pipeline, a floating point unit, hardware virtualization. and conditional branch prediction. Most instructions can be issued in pairs. It will be available as a licensable IP core.

The High Performance Spacecraft Computing Project (HPSC) is ongoing. The contract for development of the unit was let to the Boeing Company, in St. Louis. The contract value exceeds $26 million. The company is to develop the rad-hard computer based on the ARM architecture, multicore "chiplets, and associated software. Each chiplet has eight processor cores, and interfaces to memory and I/O resources. The architecture supports real-time, and parallel processing. The software environment is based on linux. Delivery of the computer will be by 2021.

Strength in numbers

As a standard ARM architecture, the NGSP will support the use of

23

standard, open source, operating systems such as linux, and applications. One relevant open source software is NASA/GSFC's Beowulf, which allows clustering. For example, a 64-node cluster computer, using the Pi architecture has already been built. The throughput is staggering. Additions to the original software allow for load leveling across the unit. The Beowulf cluster can be built from standard off-the-shelf commercial grade parts, with one rad-hard watchdog computer keeping tabs on all the compute units. It would also do trending across the cluster, and watch for pending problems that might be avoided with a timely reset.

Such as cluster computer could be utilized to support, in situ, a distributed space system, such as a swarm or constellation of Cubesats. These would be observing the same target from different points of view, or using different sensor types. The Intelligent Constellation Executive, or "mothership" would provide local management, control, and data processing for the swarm. This is a type of space-based sensor web, using multiple cooperating systems, managed locally.

ARM at work

There have been numerous space projects utilizing the ARM processor. To be used in a mission-critical application in space, the processor has to be insensitive to radiation damage. This involves both circuit-level and architectural (implementation) techniques for radiation hardening against both total dose and transient events, such as single event upsets (SEU's). These areas are fairly well understood, and techniques such as TMR (triple modular redundancy) and error detection and correction codes are employed. These techniques apply not only to the CPU, but also the memory and I/O circuitry as well.

Besides attitude determination and control, the onboard embedded system has a variety of housekeeping tasks to attend to.

Generally, there is a dedicated unit, sometimes referred to as the

Command & Data Handler (C&DH) with interfaces with the spacecraft transmitters and receivers, the onboard data storage system, and the flight computer. The C&DH, itself a computer, is in charge of uplinked data (generally, commands), onboard data storage, and data transmission. The C&DH can forward received commands directly to various spacecraft components, or can hold them for later execution at a specified time. The C&DH has a direct connection with the science instrument(s) for that data stream. If the science instrument package has many units, there may be a separate science C&DH (SC&DH) that consolidates the sensed data, and hands it over to the C&DH for transmission to the ground. It is also common for the C&DH to hand over all commands related to science instruments to the IC&DH.

Consumables inventory
The spacecraft computer can calculate and maintains a table of consumables data, both value and usage rate. This includes available state-of-charge in the batteries, amount of thruster propellant, and any other renewable or consumable asset. This is periodically telemetered to the ground.

Thermal management

The spacecraft electronics needs to be kept within a certain temperature for proper operation. Generally, the only heat source is the Sun, and the only heat sink is deep space. There are options as to how the spacecraft can be oriented. In close orbit to a planet, the planet may also represent a heat source. Automatic thermal louvers can be used to regulate the spacecraft internal temperature. The flight computer's job is to keep the science instruments or communications antennae pointed in the right direction. This might have to be overridden in the case where the spacecraft is getting too hot or too cold.

Electrical Power/energy management

The flight computer needs to know the state-of-charge (SOC) of the batteries and whether current is flowing into or out of the batteries. It the SOC is getting too low, some operations must be suspended, and the solar panels or spacecraft itself can be re-oriented to maximize charging. In some cases, redundant equipment may be turned off, according to a predetermined load-shedding algorithm. If the spacecraft batteries are fully discharged, it is generally the end of the mission, because pointing to the Sun cannot be achieved, except by lucky accident. Spacecraft going beyond Jupiter rely on RTG's – radioisotope thermoelectric generators.

Antenna Pointing

The spacecraft communications antennae must be pointed to the large antennae on the ground (Earth) or to a communications relay satellite in a higher orbit (for Earth or Mars). The Antennae can usually be steered in two axis, independently of the spacecraft body. This can be accomplished in the Main flight computer, or be a task for the C&DH.

Safe Hold mode

As a last resort, the spacecraft has a safe-hold or survival mode that operates without computer intervention. This usually seeks to orient the spacecraft with its solar panels to the Sun to maximize power, turn off all non-essential systems, and call for help. This can be implemented in a dedicated digital unit. It used to be the case that the safe-hold mode was implemented in analog circuitry.

Science Data Processing

I have not mentioned the science payload. Generally, the science instrument(s) have their own dedicated computers that collect the data and hand it over to the spacecraft Command & Data handling unit to be downlinked with the "housekeeping" data. Some level of science data processing can also be done onboard. As missions go further out, and collect more and more data, there is a need for some processing of the data onboard, which may take years (New Horizons is an example) to get back to Earth.

For heavy-duty on-board data crunching, we can use standard Raspberry PI's in a cluster architecture, linked with NASA's Beowulf software.

NASA Data Processing Levels Definition

0   Reconstructed, unprocessed instrument and payload data at full resolution, with any and all communications artifacts (e. g., synchronization frames, communications headers, duplicate data) removed.

1a   Reconstructed, unprocessed instrument data at full resolution, time-referenced, and annotated with ancillary information, including radiometric and geometric calibration coefficients and geo-referencing parameters (e. g., platform ephemeris) computed and appended but not applied to the Level 0 data (or if applied, in a manner that level 0 is fully recoverable from level 1a data).

1b   Level 1a data that have been processed to sensor units (e. g., radar backscatter cross section, brightness temperature, etc.); not all instruments have Level 1b data; level 0 data is not recoverable from level 1b data.

2   Derived geophysical variables (e. g., ocean wave height, soil moisture, ice concentration) at the same resolution and location as Level 1 source data.

3   Variables mapped on uniform spacetime grid scales, usually with some completeness and consistency (e. g., missing points interpolated, complete regions mosaic-ed together from multiple

orbits, etc.).

4   Model output or results from analyses of lower level data (i. e., variables that were not measured by the instruments but instead are derived from these measurements).

The ARM processor has found extensive usage in the area of Cubesats. A Cubesat is a small, affordable satellite that can be developed and launched by college, high schools, and even individuals. The specifications were developed by Academia in 1999. The basic structure is a 10 centimeter cube, (volume of 1 liter) weighing less that 1.33 kilograms. This allows a series of these standardized packages to be launched as secondary payloads on other missions. A Cubesat dispenser has been developed, the Poly-PicoSat Orbital Deployer, that holds multiple Cubesats and dispenses them on orbit. They can also be launched from the Space Station, via a custom airlock. ESA, the United States, and Russia provide launch services. The Cubesat origin lies with Prof. Twiggs of Stanford University and was proposed as a vehicle to support hands-on university-level space education and opportunities for low-cost space access.

Cubesats can be custom made, but there has been a major industry evolved to supply components, including space computers. It allows for an off-the-shelf implementation, in addition to the custom build. There is quite a bit of synergy between the Amsat folks and Cubesats. NASA supports the Cubesat program, holding design contests providing a free launch to worthy projects. Cubesats are being developed around the world, and several hundred have been launched.

A simple Cubesat controller can be developed from a standard embedded platform such as the Arduino. The lack of radiation hardness can be balanced by the short on-orbit lifetime. The main drivers for a Cubesat flight computer are small size, small power consumption, wide functionality, and flexibility. In addition, a wide temperature range is desirable. The architecture should support a real time operating system.

The 32-bit implementation of the Arduino architecture is a strong candidate for Cubesat onboard computers. Many implementations feature a real-time clock, which is an add-on item in the Raspberry Pi architecture. A real time clock allows for the implementation of a real-time operating system. Cubesats with Arduinos have flown in orbit. The Arduino mini on the unit from Interorbital systems incorporates a current sensor to indicate a single event upset may have occurred due to radiation. The Arduino architecture has a relatively low tolerance to radiation damage. On the International Space Station, the dual Raspberry Pi B+ based AstroPi runs student -submitted software. The units are on the ISS LAN, and can be uploaded and downloaded from the ground. They make use of WiFi and have 32G micro SD cards. Raspbian is the operating system.

Although the standard Raspberry Pi is not designed to be Rad hard, it showed a surprisingly good radiation tolerance in tests. It continued to operate through a dose of 150 krad(Si), with only the loss of USB connectivity. Several commercial cubesat flight computers are based on the ARM architecture of the Pi. When the rad-hard P emerges, the games changes significantly.

The NanoMind A712D is an onboard computer for Cubesats. It uses a 32-bit ARM cpu, with 2 megabytes of RAM, and 8 megabytes of flash memory. It can also support a MicroSD flash card. It has a Can bus and a I^2C interface. It comes with an extensive software library and real time operating system. Special applications, such as attitude determination and control code are available. It is tolerant to temperatures form -40 to 85 degrees C, but is not completely rad-hard.

The UK Space agency kicked off a project in December of 2014 called Astro Pi. It was a competition for primary and secondary schools to come up with a project and associated code for a Cubesat. Two units were taken by British Astronaut Tim Peake to the International Space Station in December of 2015. Each has a camera (one for visible spectrum, one for infrared), and each has a magnetometer as well as temperature and humidity sensors. Each unit is standard, but is housed in a purpose built aluminum case.

The PiSat is a product of the Goddard Space Flight Center. It uses a Raspberry Pi flight controller, with a battery of sensors. The case is 3D printed. The project kicked off the 2014. The software is the GSFC Core Flight System modules.

The Space environment

We'll discuss the environment in which satellites and their computers operate, assuming they survive the launch.

The space environment is hostile and non-forgiving. Is there gravity in space. Of course. It is a relationship between two masses. I the orbital case, between the satellite and the Earth. It's just that the satellite is traveling very fast, and it balances out the gravitational pull. In fact, the satellite is in the gravity field of everything else in the solar system and universe. Most of that stuff is too far away to make much difference. But, recall, the Moon effects the oceans -we call them tides. With no gravity, no convection cooling is possible, leading to potential thermal problems. Space is a high radiation environment, being above the shielding provided by Earth's atmosphere, and the magnetic field.

There are differing environments by Mission type. For Near-Earth orbiters, there are the radiation problems of the Van Allen belts and the South Atlantic Anomaly, the thermal and vacuum environment, and the issue of atmospheric drag. This drag causes orbital decay, where the spacecraft slowly descends. There is also a drag factor from the residual atmosphere and the solar wind, and the spacecraft's orbit can be affected in other ways. All Cubesat missions are currently near Earth, although NASA is developing specialized Cubesats for planetary exploration.

Zero G issues

Zero gravity, actually, free-fall, brings with it problems. There is no convection cooling, as that relies on the different densities of warm and cool air. Any little pieces of conductive material will float around and short out critical circuitry at the worst possible time. And then, there are the strange issues.

The Hughes HS 601 series of communications spacecraft suffered a series of failures in 1992-1995 due to relays. In zero gravity, tin "whiskers" grew within the units, causing them to short. The control processors on six spacecraft were effected, with three mission failures because both primary and backup computers failed. This is now a well known materials issue, with recommendations for the proper solder to be used. In 1998, the on-orbit Galaxy IV satellite's main control computer failed due to tin whiskers.

Vacuum

The Satellites operate in vacuum. Not a perfect vacuum, but fairly close. This implies a few things. Lubricants evaporate and disappear. All materials outgas to some extent. All this stuff can find its way to condense on optical surfaces, solar arrays, and radiators.

Thermal environment

In space, things are either too hot or too cold. Cooling is by conduction to an outside surface, and then radiation to cold space. This requires heat-generating electronics to have a conductive path to a radiator. That makes board design and chip packaging complex and expensive. You get about 1 watt per square meter of sunlight in low Earth orbit. This will heat up the spacecraft, or you can convert it to electrical power with solar arrays.

Parts (and you) can be damaged by excessive heat, both ambient and self-generated. In a condition known as *thermal runaway*, an uncontrolled positive feedback situation is created, where overheating causes the part to further overheat, and fail faster.

There can be a large thermal gradient of hundreds of degrees across a satellite, where one side faces the sun, and the other side faces cold space. There is a similar situation at the planet Mercury, where one side always faces the Sun, and the other, deep space. It wiggles a little, creating what is called the "Goldilocks Zone," not too hot, not too cold.

Orbital Debris

There is a huge amount of debris in Earth orbit, including old booster rockets, failed satellites (Zombie-sats), broken solar panels, nuts and bolts, a Russian Space Suit. Space is large, but all of this stuff constitutes a hazard to ongoing missions. All this stuff is tracked and reported by the U.S. Air Force. There is a requirement now that old, end-of-life satellites have to reenter the atmosphere and burn up.

Mechanical and Structural Issues

In zero gravity, everything floats, whether you want it to or not. Floating conductive particles, bits of solder or bonding wire, can short out circuitry, internal to the chip, or on boards that were not coated.

ESD sensitivity

Solid state devices are particularly susceptible to electrostatic discharge (ESD) effects. These effects can involve very large voltages that cause device breakdown. Certain semiconductor lattice structures that have been damaged can actually "heal" over time, a process called annealing. Passive parts are sensitive to ESD as well. As parts are made smaller, the susceptibility to ESD effects increases. Proper grounding helps with ESD, providing a consistent voltage across components, without significant differences. ESD lead to sudden catastrophic failure.

Spacecraft Charging

Another problem with on-orbit spacecraft is that they are not "grounded." This can be a problem when a potential develops across the structure. Ideally, steps were taken to keep every surface linked, electrically. But, the changing phenomena has been the cause of spacecraft system failures. Where does the charge come from? Mostly, the Sun, in the forms of charged particles. This can cause surface charging, and even internal charging. Above about 90 kilometers in altitude, the spacecraft is in a plasma environment At low Earth orbit, there is a low energy but high density of the plasma. The plasma rotates with the Earth's magnetic field. The density is greater at the equator, and less at the magnetic poles. Generally, electrons with energies from 1-100 keV cause surface charging, and those over 100 keV can penetrate and cause internal charging. As modern electronics is very susceptible to electron damage, proper management of charging is needed at the design level.

Just flying along in orbit causes an electric field around the spacecraft, as any conductor traveling through a magnetic field does. If everything is at the same potential, we're good, but if there's a difference in potential, there can be electrostatic discharge. These discharges lead to electronics damage and failure, and can also cause physical damage to surfaces, due to arcing. This has been a problem at the International Space Station.

Radiation effects

On Earth, we are shielded from most radiation by our atmosphere and magnetic field. The Sun is the major source of our radiation, and high-energy particles. Right now, based on International Space Station experience, an Astronaut can have a maximum duration in space of about a year, before receiving his/her maximum lifetime dose. At the ISS you get, in a day, what some one on the ground would accumulate in a year. Shielding is one answer, but it can be counter-productive. Sometimes, a hit by a massively energetic particle can cause a spray of lower energy particles, from the shielding itself.

A large solar flare occurred in September of 1859, and was observed by British astronomer R. C. Carrington in his private observatory on his estate outside of London. Both the associated sunspots and the flare were visible to the naked eye. The resulting geomagnetic storm was recorded by a magnetograph in Britain as well. They also recorded a perturbation in the Earth's ionosphere, that we now know is caused by ionizing x-rays. In 1859, this was all observed, but not understood. Even the ionosphere was not know to exist at the time. Now, we know a Coronal Mass Ejection from the sun, associated with a solar storm, is first seen as an energy burst hitting the Earth, and later by vast streams of charged particles, that travel slower than the speed of light. At normal levels, these particles are seen as the Northern or Southern lights. The Earth's magnetic field is affected.

What did happen, and was not immediately associated with the solar storm, was interference with the early telegraph systems of the time. The telegraph was relatively new, and wires stretched for many miles. Think of them as long antennas. The telegraph equipment was damaged, and large arc's of electricity started fires and shocked operators. No fatalities were reported. The employees of American Telegraph Company in New York found they could transmit messages with the batteries of their systems disconnected. The Northern lights were visible from Cuba. This was the largest such solar flare in at least 500 years...and so far.

What if such a super flare occurred today? First, we would have warning from sentinel satellites such as the Solar Dynamics Observatory, that are closer to the sun, and detect the passage of particles. They can tell us about this via radio, which travels faster than the particles. So, we would have a day or so's notice. All of our modern high-technology infrastructure would be at risk of damage, from the electrical grid to the Internet. Most of our satellites would be damaged, removing services we rely on such as long distance data communication, and navigation. It would be much better to turn everything off, and ride out the storm. Even that might not prevent major damage to networks. When is the next large solar event? Even the Astrophysicists can't tell us that.

Cumulative dose and single events

The more radiation that the equipment gets, in low doses for a long time, or in high doses for a shorter time, the greater the probability of damage.

These events are caused by high energy particles, usually protons, that disrupt and damage the semiconductor lattice. The effects can be upsets (bit changes) or latch-ups (bit stuck). The damage can "heal" itself, but its often permanent. Most of the problems are caused by energetic solar protons, although galactic cosmic rays are also an issue. Solar activity varies, but is now monitored by sentinel spacecraft, and periods of intensive solar radiation and particle flux can be predicted. Although the Sun is only 8 light minutes away from Earth, the energetic particles travel much slower than light, and we have several days warning. During periods of intense solar activity, Coronal Mass Ejection (CME) events can send massive streams of charged particles outward. These hit the Earth's magnetic field and create a bow wave. The Aurora Borealis or Northern Lights are one manifestation of incoming charged particles hitting the upper reaches of the ionosphere.

Cosmic rays, particles and electromagnetic radiation, are omni-directional, and come from extra-solar sources. Most of them, 85%, are protons with gamma rays and x-rays thrown in the mix. Energy levels range to 10^6 to 10^8 electron volts (eV). These are mostly filtered out by Earth's atmosphere. There is no such mechanism on the Moon, where they reach and interact with the surface. Solar flux energy's range to several Billion (10^9) electron volts (Gev).

The effects of radiation on silicon circuits can be mitigated by redundancy, the use of specifically radiation hardened parts, Error Detection and Correction (EDAC) circuitry, and scrubbing techniques. Hardened chips are produced on special insulating substrates such as sapphire and diamond. Bipolar technology chips can withstand radiation better than CMOS technology chips, at the cost of greatly increased power consumption. Shielding techniques are also applied. Even a small thickness of aluminum blocks many of the energetic particles. However, a problem occurs when a particle collides with the aluminum atoms, creating a cascade of lower energy particles that can also cause damage. In error detection and correction techniques, special encoding of the stored information provides a protection against flipped bits, at the cost of additional bits to store. Redundancy can also be applied at the device or box level, with the popular Triple Modular Redundancy (TMR) technique triplicating everything, and assuming the probability of a double failure is less than that of a single failure. Watchdog timers are used to reset systems unless they are themselves reset by the software. Of course, the watchdog timer circuitry is also susceptible to failure.

Spacecraft computer systems followed the trend from purpose-built custom units to those based on standard microprocessors. However, the space environment is very unforgiving in many areas, the chief one being radiation. Commercial electronic parts may not last very long in orbit.

So, we have seen control systems for spacecraft go from hardwired logic to a general purpose CPU architecture programmed with software. ASIC's, or Application Specific Integrated Circuits, are also produced in radiation hard versions. This is sort of a throw-back to the hardwired approach, but has its advantages. The next step is systems built from inherently rad-hard FPGA's or chips. This brings along a penalty in price, and speed. This is the approach that is being pursued by Boeing for NASA and the Air Force.

Rad-Hard Software

From formal testing results, and key engineering tools, we define likely failure modes, and possible remediation's. Besides self-test, we will have cross-checking of systems. Not everything can be tested by the software, without some additional hardware. First, we use engineering analysis that will help us define the possible hardware and software failure cases, and then define actions and remediation. This is a software FMEA, failure modes and effects analysis. None of this is new, and the approach is to collect together best practices in the software testing area, develop a library of RHS routines, and get operational experience. Another advantage of the software approach is that we can change it after launch, as more is learned, and conditions change. If we have a cluster computer, we can do trending.

Watchdog Core

For implementations in an FPGA, a separate watchdog unit can be provided in hardware. This will have the same radiation tolerance as the main computer but will be less complex, thus have a smaller cross-section for charged particles. This section can use the TMR approach, rather than the entire chip. This approach was implemented by SiFive in their

FE301 and FE540, their fourth generation flash-based FPGA chip. They are immune to radiation-induced changes to configuration.

The FPGA fabric has 150,000 logic cells, which can implement math blocks, micro (64x18) and large (1024x18) SRAM, They support dual 667 mbps DDR ports.

These parts have a flight heritage. They are manufactured in a 65 nm process. They are qualified to a MIL-STD-883, Class B spec. They support JTAG, as well as 16 Spacewire ports., and PCI Express.

The advantage of having a inherently rad-hard device that can be instantiated with the VHDL for a ARM architecture, is that you now have a rad-hard ARM. However, you have to buy an ARM architecture license first.

Radiation Damage Mitigation

Homeostasis refers to a system that monitors, corrects, and controls its own state. Our bodies do that with our blood pressure, temperature, blood sugar level, and many other parameters.

We can have the spacecraft computer monitor its own performance, or have two identical systems monitor each other. Each approach has problems. We can also choose to "triplicate" the hardware, and use external logic to see if results differ. The idea is, two outweigh one, because the probability of a double error is less than that of a single error.

In at least one case I know of, the backup computer erroneously thought the primary made a mistake, and took over control. It was wrong, and caused a spacecraft failure.

To counter the effects of "bit flips" and other effects of radiation, the memory can be designed with error detection and correction (EDAC). Generally, this means a longer, encoded word that can detect and correct M errors. There is a trade-off with price. With EDAC memory, there is a low priority background task running on the cpu that continuously reading and writing back to memory. This process, called "memory scrubbing" will catch and correct errors.

Open Source versus Proprietary

This is a topic we need to discuss before we get too far into software. It is not a technical topic, but concerns your right to use (and/or own) software. It's those software licenses you click to agree with, and never read. That's what the intellectual property lawyers are betting on.

Software and software tools are available in proprietary and open source versions. *Open source software* is free and widely available, and may be incorporated into your system. It is available under license, which generally says that you can use it, but derivative products must be made available under the same license. This presents a problem if it is mixed with purchased, licensed commercial software, or a level of exclusivity is required. Major government agencies such as the Department of Defense and NASA have policies related to the use of Open Source software.

Adapting a commercial or open source operating system to a particular problem domain can be tricky. Usually, the commercial operating systems need to be used "as-is" and the source code is not available. The software can usually be configured between well-defined limits, but there will be no visibility of the internal workings. For the open source situation, there will be a multitude of source code modules and libraries that can be configured and customized, but the process is complex. The user can also write new modules in this case.

Large corporations or government agencies sometimes have problems incorporating open source products into their projects. Open Source did not fit the model of how they have done business traditionally. They are issues and lingering doubts. NASA has created an open source license, the NASA Open Source Agreement (NOSA), to address these issues. It has released software under this license, but the Free Software Foundation has some issues with the terms of the license. The Open Source Initiative (www.opensource.org) maintains the definition of Open Source, and certifies licenses such as the NOSA.

The GNU General Public License (GPL) is the most widely used free software license. It guarantees end users the freedoms to use, study, share, copy, and modify the software. Software that ensures that these rights are retained is called free software. The license was originally written by Richard Stallman of the Free Software Foundation (FSF) for the GNU project in 1989. The GPL is a copyleft license, which means that derived works can only be distributed under the same license terms. This is in distinction to permissive free software licenses, of which the BSD licenses are the standard examples. Copyleft is in counterpoint to traditional copyright. Proprietary software "poisons" the free software, and cannot be included or integrated with it, without abandoned the GPL. The GPL cover the GNU/linux operating systems and most of the GNU/linux-based applications.

A Vendor's software tools and Operating system or application code is usually also proprietary intellectual property. It is unusual to get the source code to examine, at least without binding legal documents and additional funds. Along with this, you get the vendor support. Open Source describes a collaborative environment for development and testing. Use of open source code carries with it an implied responsibility to "pay back" to the community. Open Source is not necessarily free.

The Open source philosophy is sometimes at odds with the rigidtized procedures evolved to ensure software performance and reliability. Offsetting this is the increased visibility into the internals of the software packages, and control over the entire software package. Besides application code, operating systems such as GNU/linux and bsd can be open source. The programming language Python is open source, as is the popular web server Apache, and the data base MySQL.

ARM Flight software

This section discuss the software, both application code and operating systems. All spacecraft are run by on-board computers that implement the various tasks. A set of common spacecraft functions has been implements in an open-source library from NASA's Goddard Space Flight Center, Flight Software Branch. This is called the Core Flight Software. It runs under the Core Flight Executive (cFE).

The ARM architecture can host the open source Fedora linux, Debian, Gentoo, FreeBSD, NetBSD, BuildRoot (embedded). The executive is a set of mission independent reusable software services and an operating environment. Within this architecture, various mission-specific applications can be hosted. The cFE focuses on the commonality of flight software. The Core Flight System (CFS) supplies libraries and applications. Decades of flight software legacy went into the concept of the cFE. Various modules provide functions such as command and telemetry service, scheduling, limit checking,and file delivery in CCSDS format.

Linux

Linux is an open source operating system. There are actually a series of different versions of Linux. Like all operating systems, it is designed to manage computer resources – memory, programs, I/O. It handles these for desktop and server computers. The standard version does not support real-time applications. A version called RTLinux can be used, and various other non-linux or linux-like operating systems are available for real-time applications. Linux was developed and is managed by Linus Torvalds, a Finnish software engineer. Popular operating systems such as Chrome and Android are derived from Linux.

Real time operating systems still manage computer resources, but the most important thing they manage is timing. Besides Linux, BSD (Berkeley Systems Distribution version of Bell Labs Unix) is another choice. This was developed and is maintained by the University of California, Berkeley. There are many variations of BSD. Another popular real time, open source operating system is RTEMS.

cFE/cFS

The Core Flight Executive, from the Flight Software Branch, Code 582, at NASA/GSFC, is an open source operating system framework. The executive is a set of mission independent reusable software services and an operating environment. Within this architecture, various mission-specific applications can be hosted. The cFE focuses on the commonality of flight software. The Core Flight System (cFS) supplies libraries and applications. Much flight software legacy went into the concept of the cFE. It has gotten traction within the Goddard community, and is in use on many flight projects, simulators, and test beds (FlatSats) at multiple NASA centers. The code library is managed by the Goddard Space Flight Center, and, being open source, submissions from outside sources are tested and accepted

The cFE presents a layered architecture, starting with the bootstrap process, and including a real time operating system. At this level, a board support package is needed for the particular hardware in use. Many of these have been developed. At the OS abstraction level, a Platform support package is included. The cFE core comes next, with cFE libraries and specific mission libraries. Ap's are the 5th, or upper layer. The cFE strives to provide a platform and project independent run time environment.

The boot process involves software to get things going after power-on, and is contained in non-volatile memory. cFE has boot loaders for ARM as well as other architectures. The real time operating systems can be any of a number of different open source or proprietary products, VxWorks and RTEMS for example. This layer provides interrupt handling, a scheduler, a file system, and inter-process communication.

The Platform Support Package is an abstraction layer that allows the cFE to run a particular RTOS on a particular hardware platform. There is a PSP for desktop pc's for the cFE. The cFE Core includes a set of re-usable, mission independent services. It presents a standardized application Program Interface (API) to the programmer. A software bus architecture is provided for messaging between applications.

The Event services at the core level provides an interface to send asynchronous messages, telemetry. The cFE also provides time services.

Aps include a Health and Safety Ap with a watchdog. A housekeeping AP for messages with the ground, data storage and file manager aps, a memory checker, a stored command processor, a scheduler, a checksummer, and a memory manager. Aps can be developed and added to the library with ease.

A recent NASA/GSFC Cubesat project uses a FPGA-based system-on-a-chip architecture with Linux and the cFE. The cFE has been released into the World-Wide Open Source community, and has found many applications outside of NASA.

NASA's Software Architecture Review Board considered the cFE in 2011. They found it a well thought-out product that definitely met a NASA need. It was also seen to have the potential of becoming a dominant flight software architectural framework. The technology was seen to be mature.

The cFS is the core flight software, a series of aps for generally useful tasks onboard the spacecraft. The cFS is a platform and project independent reusable software framework and set of reusable applications. This framework is used as the basis for the flight software for satellite data systems and instruments, but can be used on other embedded systems in general. More information on the cFS can be found at http://cFS.gsfc.nasa.gov

OSAL
The OS Abstraction Layer (OSAL) project is a small software library that isolates the embedded software from the real time operating system. The OSAL provides an Application Program Interface (API) to an abstract real time operating system. This provides a way to develop one set of embedded application code that is independent of the operating system being used. It is a form of middleware.

cFS aps

cFS aps are core Flight System (cFS) applications that are plug-in's to the Core Flight Executive (cFE) component. Some of these are discussed below.

CCSDS File Delivery (CF)

The CF application is used for transmitting and receiving files. To transfer files using CFDP, the CF application must communicate with a CFDP compliant peer. CF sends and receives file information and file-data in Protocol Data Units (PDUs) that are compliant with the CFDP standard protocol defined in the CCSDS 727.0-B-4 Blue Book. The PDUs are transferred to and from the CF application via CCSDS packets on the cFE's software bus middleware.

Limit check (LC)

The LC application monitors telemetry data points in a cFS system and compares the values against predefined threshold limits. When a threshold condition is encountered, an event message is issued and a Relative Time Sequence (RTS) command script may be initiated to respond/react to the threshold violation.

Checksum (CS)

The CS application is used for for ensuring the integrity of onboard memory. CS calculates Cyclic Redundancy Checks (CRCs) on the different memory regions and compares the CRC values with a baseline value calculated at system start up. CS has the ability to ensure the integrity of cFE applications, cFE tables, the cFE core, the onboard operating system (OS), onboard EEPROM, as well as, any memory regions ("Memory") defined by the users.

Stored Command (SC)

The SC application allows a system to be autonomously commanded 24 hours a day using sequences of commands that are loaded to SC. Each command has a time tag associated with it, permitting the command to be released for distribution at predetermined times. SC supports both Absolute Time tagged command Sequences (ATSs) as well as multiple Relative Time tagged command Sequences (RTSs).

Scheduler (SCH)

The SCH application provides a method of generating software bus messages at pre-determined timing intervals. This allows the system to operate in a Time Division Multiplexed (TDM) fashion with deterministic behavior. The TDM major frame is defined by the Major Time Synchronization Signal used by the cFE TIME Services (typically 1 Hz). The Minor Frame timing (number of slots executed within each Major Frame) is also configurable.

File Manager (FM)

The FM application provides onboard file system management services by processing ground commands for copying, moving, and renaming files, decompressing files, creating directories, deleting files and directories, providing file and directory informational telemetry messages, and providing open file and directory listings. The FM requires use of the cFS application library.

Data Storage (DS)

The DS application is used for storing software bus messages in files. These files are generally stored on a storage device such as a solid state recorder but they could be stored on any file system. Another cFS application such as CFDP (CF) must be used in order to transfer the files created by DS from their onboard storage location to where they will be viewed and processed. DS requires use of the cFS application library.

Memory Manager (MM)

The MM application is used for the loading and dumping system memory. MM provides an operator interface to the memory manipulation functions contained in the PSP (Platform Support Package) and OSAL (Operating System Abstraction Layer) components of the cFS. MM provides the ability to load and dump memory via command parameters, as well as, from files. Supports symbolic addressing. MM requires use of the cFS application library.

Housekeeping (HK)

The HK application is used for building and sending combined telemetry messages (from individual system applications) to the software bus for routing. Combining messages is performed in order to minimize downlink telemetry bandwidth. Combined messages are also useful for organizing certain types of data packets together. HK provides the capability to generate multiple combined packets so that data can be sent at different rates.

Memory Dwell (MD)

The MD application monitors memory addresses accessed by the CPU. This task is used for both debugging and monitoring unanticipated telemetry that had not been previously defined in the system prior to deployment. The MD application requires use of the cFS application library .

Software Bus Network (SBN)

The SBN application extends the cFE Software Bus (SB) publish/subscribe messaging service across partitions, processes, processors, and networks. The SBN is prototype code and requires a patch to the cFE Software Bus code. This is now included in the software library.

Health and Safety (HS)

The HS application provides functionality for Application Monitoring, Event Monitoring, Hardware Watchdog Servicing, Execution Counter Reporting (optional), and CPU Aliveness Indication (via UART).

Being open source, you can write your own cFS aps for specific applications, or modify existing ones. However, you should submit them back to the owner (NASA-GSFC) for review and validation so they become a part of the official package.

One particularly useful approach to storing data onboard is to use Electronic Data sheets, a standard for device and event description. For example, we might have an EDS for a battery, holding the temperature, voltage, and state of charge in a standardized format. There EDS's can then easily be held in a database, such as the open -source SQL-lite. This simplifies accessing an item in the database.

ARM Application Software

In the area of applications software and development, there is a natural synergy between Java and the ARM architecture. This is not to say that other languages such as c/c++ can't be used. A c language to byte code compiler exists, as does those for other languages. An ARM implementation does not need to support the ARM ISA, strangely enough. Data access is little- or big endian, with little-endian the default. The processor view of memory is that it is a linear structure of bytes, numbered in ascending order from zero. Supported data types include 8, 16, and 32-bit words. A programmer's view of the registers shows R0-R12 as general purpose, R13 as the stack pointer, R14 as the link register, and R15 as the program counter. R8 to R12 are not accessible by 16-bit instructions.

Numerous software tools and environments for the ARM exist, both proprietary and open source. These include tools from industry leaders such as Wind River (VxWorks), Green Hills, Mentor Graphics, QNX, and others. These are both development and debugging toolsets. Keil provides a software development environment for ARM, and ARM itself has a "development studio" for the chips.

Data Bases, and Electronic Data Sheets

Databases are useful for organizing data, and making it easy to access. The are many excellent database products, usually based on the Structured Query Language (SQL) model. The incoming telemetry and outgoing commands are stored, time tagged. There is no need to re-invent the wheel again here. Commercial databases (and some come in open source versions) scale well and provide the security and query features needed. SQL is the linux-based product of choice, with the SQLlite slimmed down version applicable to spacecraft onboard use.

Telemetry data, or observation data organized into Electronic Data Sheets can be stored in the onboard database. EDS's provide a structure to the characteristics and device description data.

Beowulf

The Beowulf open source clustering software was developed at NASA's Goddard Space Flight Center. It allowed the use of commodity pc's to be used in the construction of a large parallel processor. The pc's would generally be using the linux operating system, although BSD will work. Generally, the nodes would be identical. The Message Passing Interface (MPI), and Parallel Virtual Machine software libraries are used. The original project was defined in 1998, and the units are now used world wide as an inexpensive high-end supercomputer. Beowulf clusters automatically link together at boot time, needing no particular configuration. The architecture is scalable to whatever number of computers you want, more dependent on floor space, electrical power, and cooling. 64 nodes are common.

Now, think about linking 64 Raspberry-Pi computers into a cluster. It's been done. Since the Pi's cost around $35, you have the computer architecture of a 64-node machine for around $2500. You need the networking infrastructure to link all those machines together as well, using ethernet over USB.

What is such a cluster good at? Crunching large amounts of data. With a Rad-hard Pi cluster onboard the spacecraft, large amounts of data can be examined at the source. Another, less-expensive approach is to use COTS Pi units, with a Rad-hard watchdog, which could be a rad-hard Arduino architecture, of which there are currently several.

A Rad-Hard ARM Cortex-M0 is a microcontroller from Protec GmbH, a company with 30 years experience in rad-hard electronics, and a portfolio of processor and support parts. It provides a Cortex M0 cpu, operating at 50 Mhz, and using 3.3 volts. Memory includes 16k each of data and program memory. Error detection and correction is included. It can interface with up to 36 megabytes of external memory. It includes GPIO pins, that can also be used as interrupts. There are 32 general purpose counter-timers, and dual UARTS. There are dual SPI interfaces.

All internal registers are triple-modular redundant. It is hardened to a TID of 300 krad, and is latch-up immune to 100 MeV-cm^2/mg. It comes in a 1.3 x 1.3 inch, 188 pin package. Not a computational powerhouse, it is a capable controller.

The SAMRH71 is a rad-hard-by-design microcontroller chip from Microchip, based on their commercial grade SAMv71. It is a 32-bit Cortex M7. The rad hard version includes Spacewire and MIL-STD-1553 I/O. The radiation performance is a LET of 62 MeV/CM^2 with an SEU greater than 20 and a TID of 100 Krad. This microcontroller operates up to 100 MHz. Besides the rad-hard part, a less-expensive radiation-tolerant part is also available. The part includes CAN and Ethernet interfaces.

Vorago Technologies is marketing the VA10820, an ARM Cortex-M0 that is hard to 300krad. It operates at 50 MHz, and includes JTAG. It has 32k of data memory, and 128k of program memory. Memory EDAC and scrub are included. It is a microcontroller, with 54 GPIO's, dual i2c, dual UART, and triple SPI's. It has a remarkable 24 32-bit counter-timers, and includes PWM's, and a watchdog timer. All internal registers are TMR.

The Atmega S-128 is a rad-hard microcontroller, with the Cortex M7 architecture. It has Spacewire and 1553 bus. It can work up to a total integrated dose of 100 Krad.

What type of algorithm would we run on the cluster? One example is the PNN – probabilistic neural net. This open source software is good at classification and uncovering patterns in data sets. The

PNN model has four layers, the input, the pattern, the summation, and the output. PNN's have been proven to be fast and accurate. A large amount of memory space is required to store the model.

What Space Missions use ARM?

The Surrey Satellite Technology Nanosat Applications Platform (SNAP-1) was launched on June 28, 2000. The onboard computer (OBC) is based on Intel's StrongArm SA-1100 with 4 Mbytes of 32-bit wide EDAC protected SRAM. The error correction logic can correct 2 bits in every 8 using a modified Hamming code and the errors are "washed" from memory by software to prevent accumulation from multiple single-event upsets. There is 2 Mbytes of Flash memory containing a simple bootloader which loads the application software into SRAM.

The NanoMind A712D is an onboard computer for Cubesats. It uses as 32-bit ARM cpu, with 2 megabytes of RAM, and 8 megabytes of flash memory. It can also support a MicroSD flash card. It has a Can bus and a I²C interface. It comes with an extensive software library and real time operating system. Special applications, such as attitude determination and control code are available. It is tolerant to temperatures form -40 to 85 degrees C, but is not completely rad-hard.

Mars Helicopter Scout

The next Mars mission in 2021 will include the 2020 Rover, which has a robotic helicopter. It will be an eye-in-the-sky, looking out for hazards, planning a path, and see things that the rover's camera can't. It will be autonomous in operation. It is a technology demonstration, planned to fly five times, during the early mission. The copter blades are a meter in diameter, and it has two counter-rotating sets. Compasses can't work on Mars due to the low magnetic field, so it will use solar tracking and inertial guidance. It will have its own solar panels. It is carried under the rover. It is dropped to the ground, and the rover moves some distance away so it can ascend. It runs linux.

Cosmos

The open source control center software (COSMOS, from Ball Aerospace) can be hosted on a Raspberry Pi class machine. A student team, headed by the author, modified it slightly to provide telemetry data from the cubesat directly an Apache web server, running on the same host machine. The telemetry data, once posted on the website, could be accessed by other computers over the web, and by tablets and smart phones.

More interestingly, COSMOS can be hosted on a ARM architecture in a mothership, giving local control of a constellation or swarm. The one addition to the standard COSMOS product is an agent module, a virtual flight controller. This module makes decisions and takes appropriate action for the smaller units, in the scenario where the ground-based control center is not in communication. One advantage of this approach is that the controller can "learn" which actions were appropriate and effective, and modify its behavior accordingly. In a mission scenario I worked on, the swarm was on the opposite side of the Sun, from the Earth, so there were long periods of a lack of communications. This meant that the swarm had to be managed locally. This is what can be used for in-site constellation management and control.

Afterword

The game is changing. With the advent of rad-hard Arduino-class microcontrollers, and the development of a Rad-hard, Raspberry-Pi class ARM, the options for computation on smallsats has expanded. This is facilitated by the use of available, open-source software.

Glossary of Terms

1553 – Military standard data bus, serial, 1 Mbps.

1U – one unit for a Cubesat, 10 x 10 x 10 cm.

3U – three units for a Cubesat.

ACE – attitude control electronics.

A/D – analog to digital

AFRL – Air Force Research Laboratory.

ALU – arithmetic logic unit.

AMBA – (ARM) Advanced Microcontroller Bus Architecture.

ANSI – American National Standards Institute.

ANTS – Autonomous NanoTechnology Swarm..

AP – application programs.

API – application program interface; specification for software modules to communicate.

Arduino – a small, inexpensive microcontroller architecture.

ARM – originally, Acorn RISC Machine; later Advanced RISC Machine.

ASIC – Application Specific Integrated Circuit.

Baud – symbol rate; may or may not be the same as bit rate.

Beowulf – a clustering technique and software for commodity computers.

Big-endian – data format with the most significant bit or byte at the lowest address, or transmitted first.

Bootloader – initial program run after power-on or reset. Gets the computer up & going.

Bootstrap – a startup or reset process that proceeds without external intervention.

BSD – Berkeley Software Distribution version of the Bell Labs Unix operating system.

BP - bundle protocol, for dealing with errors and disconnects.

BSD – Berkeley System Distribution (of Unix). Open Source.

BSP – board support package. Customization Software and device drivers.

Buffer – a temporary holding location for data.

C – programming language from Bell Labs, circa 1972.

Cache – temporary storage between cpu and main memory.

Cache coherency – process to keep the contents of multiple caches consistent.

CAN – controller area network.

C&DH – Command & Data Handling.

cFE – Core Flight Executive – NASA GSFC reusable flight software.

CFS – NASA Core Flight Software, Open Source.

Chip – integrated circuit component.

Chiplet – architecture of the HPSC ARM module

Clock – periodic timing signal to control and synchronize operations.

Cluster – A group of similar units working together, satellites, computers, etc.

CODEC – coder/decoder.

Configware – equivalent of software for FPGA architectures; configuration information.

Constellations – a group of satellites.

COP – computer operating properly.

Coprocessor – another processor to supplement the operations of the main processor. Used for floating point, video, etc. Usually relies on the main processor for instruction fetch; and control.

Copyleft – an open source license applied to software or hardware.

Core – processor unit.

COSMOS – open source control Center and testing software, runs under linux.

CPU – central processing unit.

Cubesat – small inexpensive satellite for colleges, high schools, and individuals.

D/A digital to analog.

Database – an ordered collection of data.

D-cache – data cache.

DDR – dual data rate memory.

DMA – direct memory access.

DoD – (U.S.) Department of Defense.

DRAM – Dynamic random access memory.
DSP – digital signal processing/processor.
DTN – delay tolerant network
DUT – device under test.
ECC – error correcting code
EDAC – error detection and correction.
EDS – electronic data sheet.
Embedded system – a computer systems with limited human
    interfaces and performing specific tasks. Usually part of a
    larger system.
EMC – electromagnetic compatibility.
EMI – electromagnetic interference.
EOL – end of life.
FPGA – field programmable gate array
FPU – floating point unit
EDA – Exploratory Data Analysis.
EDAC – Error Detection and correction.
EDS – electronic data sheets.
EEPROM – Electrically Erasable programmable Memory (read-
    only)
FDC – fault detection and correction.
FlightLinux – NASA Research Program for Open Source code in
    space.
Floating point – computer numeric format for real numbers; has
    significant digits and an exponent.
FPGA – Field Programmable Gate Array,
FPU – floating point unit.
FRAM – ferromagnetic RAM; a non-volatile memory technology.
FTP – file transfer protocol
GEO – Geosynchronous Earth orbit.
GNC – Guidance, aviation, & Control.
GOPS – giga operations per second.
GPIO – general purpose input-output.
GNC – guidance, navigation, and control.
Gnu – recursive acronym, gnu is not unix.
GPIO – general purpose I/O.
GPL – gnu public license used for free software; referred to as the

"copyleft."

GPU - Graphics Processing Unit

GSFC – (NASA) Goddard Space Flight Center.

Handshake – co-ordination mechanism.

HDL – hardware description language.

HPCC – High Performance Computing and Communications.

HPSC – High Performance Spaceflight Computing.

Hypervisor – management of virtual domains; virtual machine monitor.

I-cache – Instruction cache.

ICD – interface control document.

IC&DH – Instrument Command & Data Handling.

IDE – Integrated Development Environment

IEEE – Institute of Electrical and Electronic engineers

IEEE-754 – standard for floating point representation and calculation.

IIC – inter-integrated circuit (I/O).

IP – intellectual property; Internet protocol.

IP core – IP describing a chip design that can be licensed to be used in an FPGA or ASIC.

IP-in-Space – Internet Protocol in Space.

ISA – instruction set architecture, the software description of the computer.

ISR – interrupt service routine, a subroutine that handles an interrupt.

I&T – integration & test.

Jazelle – (Arm) direct Java byte code execution.

JPL – (NASA) Jet Propulsion Lab of the University of California.

JVM – Java virtual machine.

Kernel – main portion of the operating system. Interface between the applications and the hardware.

Krad – kilo (10^3) rad.

Latchup – condition in which a semiconductor device is stuck in one state.

LEO – low Earth orbit.

LET – linear energy transfer.

Linux – an operating source operating system.

List – a data structure.

Little-endian – data format with the least significant bit or byte at the highest address, or transmitted last.

LRU – least recently used; an algorithm for item replacement in a cache.

MCM – MultiChip Module.

Memory leak – when a program uses memory resources but does not return them, leading to a lack of available memory.

MeV – Million (10^6) electron volts.

Microcomputer – small computer. Like what's in your phone.

Microcontroller – a cpu used with sensors and actuators, usually running real-time.

Microkernel – operating system which is not monolithic; functions execute in user space.

MIL-STD-1553 – a data communication standard for a serial bus.

MMU – memory management unit.

MPE - media processing engine.

MPI – message passing interface for cluster computers.

MPU – memory protection unit.

MRAM – Magnetorestrictive Random Access Memory.

Multicore – multiple processing cores on one substrate or chip; need not be identical.

Mutex – a software mechanism to provide mutual exclusion between tasks.

NASA – (U. S.) National Aeronautics and Space Administration.

Neon – SIMD extension for ARM

NGSP – Next Generation space Processor.

NSR – non-space rated.

NVM – non-volatile memory.

NVRAM – Nonvolatile Random access memory.

OBC – on board computer.

OBD – On-Board diagnostics.

OBP – On Board Processor.

Off-the-shelf – commercially available; not custom.

Open source – methodology for hardware or software development with free distribution and access.

OpenGL – open (source) Graphics Library.

Operating system – software that controls the allocation of resources in a computer.

OSAL – operating system abstraction layer.

Paradigm – a pattern or model

Paradigm shift – a change from one paradigm to another. Disruptive or evolutionary.

PCIE – Peripheral Component Interconnect Express (interface).

Pixel – picture element; smallest addressable element on a display or a sensor.

PNN – probabilistic neural net.

POSIX – IEEE standard operating system.

PSP – Platform Support Package.

PVM – parallel virtual machine.

Rad - unit of radiation exposure

Rad-hard – hardened to resist radiation damage.

Ram – random access memory-mapped.

RapidIO – packet switched interconnect.

Real-time – system that responds to events in a predictable, bounded time.

Register – temporary storage location for a data item.

Reset – signal and process that returns the hardware to a known, defined state.

RISC – reduced instruction set computer

RISC-v – A MIPS-based open source processor architecture.

RTOS – real time operating system.

SCP – Self-checking pairs.

SDR – software defined radio.

SDVF – Software Development and Validation Facility.

SEB – single event burnout.

SEU – single event upset.

SEL – single event latchup.

SEL – single event latchup.

SEU – single event upset (radiation induced error).

SIMD – single instruction, multiple data.

SMP – symmetric multiprocessing.

SoC – system on a chip; satellite on a chip.

SOI – silicon on insulator

SoS – silicon on sapphire – an inherently radiation-hard technology

SPW - Spacewire - high speed (160 Mbps) link.

SPI - Serial Peripheral Interface - a synchronous serial communication interface.

SQL – structured query language (for databases)

SRAM – Static Random Access Memory.

SRIO – serial rapid I/O.

SSR – solid state recorder.

Synchronous – using the same clock to coordinate operations.

System – a collection of interacting elements and relationships with a specific behavior.

System of Systems – a complex collection of systems with pooled resources.

Swarm – a collection of satellites that can operate cooperatively.

sync – synchronize, synchronized.

Thread – smallest independent set of instructions managed by a multiprocessing operating system.

Thumb (Arm) – 16 bit encoding of a subset of Arm instructions.

TID – total ionizing dose.

Thumb – 16 bit subset of ARM.

TID – total integrated dose.

TMR – triple modular redundancy

Train - – a series of satellites in the same or similar orbits, providing sequential observations.

Trust Zone – ARM security extensions.

Triplicate – using three copies (of hardware, software, messaging, power supplies, etc.). for redundancy and error control.

TRL – technology readiness level

UART – Universal Asynchronous Receiver Transmitter.

USB – universal serial bus.

VHDL – very high level design language.

Virtual memory – memory management technique using address translation.

Virtualization – creating a virtual resource from available physical resources.

VMC – vehicle management computer.

Watchdog – hardware/software function to sanity check the
hardware, software, and process; applies corrective action if
a fault is detected; fail-safe mechanism.

Zombie-sat – a dead satellite, in orbit.

References

Andrews, J. *Co-verification of Hardware and Software for ARM SoC Design*, 1st edition, 2004, Newnes, ISBN 9780080476902, ASIN: B001464118.

Atheshian, Peter and Zulaica, Daniel *ARM Synthesizable Design with Actel FPGAs: With Mixed-Signal SOC Applications*, 2010, McGraw-Hill Professional, ISBN 0071622810.

Badawy, Wael and Jullien, Graham *System-on-chip for Real-time Applications*. 2003, Kluwer, ISBN 1-4020-7254-6.

Barlas, Gerassimos *Multicore and GPU Programming: An Integrated Approach,* Morgan Kaufmann, 1st ed, 2014, ISBN-978-0124171374.

Challa, Obulapathi N., McNair, Janise "Distributed Data Storage on Cubesat Clusters," Advances in Computing 2013, (3) 3 pp.36-49. avail: http://article.sapub.org/10.5923.j.ac.20130303.02.html

Clark, P. E.; et al *BEES for ANTS: Space Mission Application for the Autonomous NanoTechnology Swarm,* avail: https://arc.aiaa.org/doi/abs/10.2514/6.2004-6303.

Furber, Stephen B. *ARM System-on-Chip Architecture* (2nd Edition), 2000, Addison Wesley Professional, ISBN 9780201675191.

Furber, Stephen B. *ARM System Architecture*, 1996 Addison-Wesley, ISBN 0201403528.

Ghahroodi. Massoud M., Ozer, Emre, Bull, David SEU and SET-tolerant ARM Cortex-R4 CPU for Space and Avionics Applications, avail: www.median-project.eu/wp-content/.../median2013_submission_5.pdf

Hall, John "maddog"; Gropp, William *Beowulf Cluster Computing with Linux*, 2003, ISBN -0262692929.

Hinchey, Michael G. ; Rash, James L.; Truszkowski, Walter E.; Rouff, Christopher A., Sterritt, Roy *Autonomous and Autonomic Swarms,* avail:
https://ntrs.nasa.gov/search.jsp?R=20050210015 2017-12-20T20:19:24+00:00Z

Jagger, Dave *ARM Architecture Reference Manual*, 1997, Prentice Hall, ISBN 0137362994.

Lamie, Edward *Real-Time Embedded Multithreading Using ThreadX and ARM*, Newnes; 2nd edition, 2009, ISBN 1856176010.

Lindberg, Van, *Intellectual Property and Open Source, A Practical Guide to Protecting Code*, 2008, O'Reilly Media, ISBN 0596517963.

Nicholson, J. *Starting Embedded GNU/linux Development on an ARM Architecture,* 1st ed., Newnes, Jul 2013, ISBN 9780080982366.

Patterson, David A and Hennessy, John L. *Computer Organization and Design: The Hardware/Software Interface*, ARM Edition, Morgan Kaufmann, 2011, ISBN 8131222748.

Predko, Michael *Programming and Customizing the ARM7 Microcontroller*, 2011, McGraw-Hill/Tab, ISBN 0071597573.

Schulte-Ladbeck, Dr. Regina E. *Basics of Spaceflight for Space Exploration, Space Commercialization, and Space Colonization,* 2016, ISBN-150252595X.

Seal, David ARM *Architecture Reference Manual,* 2nd Edition, 2001 Addison Wesley, ISBN 0201737191.

Sloss, Andrew; Symes, Dominic; and Wright, Chris *ARM System Developer's Guide: Designing and Optimizing System Software*, Morgan Kaufmann Series in Computer Architecture and Design, 2004, ISBN 9781558608740.

Specht, D. F. (1990). "Probabilistic neural networks".Neural Networks.3: 109–118.doi:10.1016/0893-6080(90)90049-Q.

St. Laurent, Andrew M. *Understanding Open Source and Free Software Licensing*, 2004, O'Reilly, ISBN- 0596005814.

Stakem, Patrick H. *The History of Spacecraft Computers from the V-2 to the Space Station*, 2013, PRRB Publishing, ISBN-1520216181.

Stakem, Patrick H. *Microprocessors in Space*, 2011, PRRB Publishing, ISBN-1520216343.

Stakem, Patrick H. *Embedded in Space,* 2015, PRRB Publishing, ISBN-1520215916.

Stakem, Patrick H. *Cubesat Engineering*, PRRB Publishing, 2017, ISBN-1520754019.

Stakem, Patrick H. Cubesat Constellations, Clusters, and Swarms, Stakem, PRRB Publishing, 2017, ISBN-1520767544.
Stakem, Patrick H. *Cubesat Operations*, PRRB Publishing, 2017, ISBN-152076717X.

Truszkowski, Walt, et al *Autonomous and Autonomic Systems: With Applications to NASA Intelligent Spacecraft Operations and Exploration Systems*, Springer, 1st Edition 2009, ISBN-1846282322.

Truszkowski, Walt; Clark, P. E.;, Curtis, S.; Rilee, M. Marr, G. "ANTS: Exploring the Solar System with an Autonomous

Nanotechnology Swarm," J. Lunar and Planetary Science XXXIII (2002).

Truszkowski, Walt "Prototype Fault Isolation Expert System for Spacecraft Control," N87-29136, avail: https://ntrs.nasa.gov/search.jsp?R=19870019703,

Valvano, Jonathan W. *Embedded Systems: Introduction to the ARM Cortex-M3*, CreateSpace Independent Publishing Platform, May 26, 2012, ISBN 1477508996.

Valvano, Jonathan W. *Embedded systems: Real time Interfacing to the ARM Cortex-M3,* CreateSpace Independent Publishing Platform, 2010, ISBN-10: 1463590156.

Valvano, Jonathan W. *Embedded systems: Real-Time Operating systems for the ARM Cortex-M3,* CreateSpace Independent Publishing Platform, January 3, 2012, ISBN-10: 1466468866.

Van Someren, Alex and Atack, Carol, *ARM RISC Chip: A Programmer's Guide*, 1994 Addison Wesley, ISBN 0201624109.

Violette, Daniel P. "Arduino/Raspberry Pi: Hobbyist Hardware and Radiation Total Dose Degradation, EEE Parts for Small Missions," GSFC, 2014, avail: https://ntrs.nasa.gov/search.jsp?R=20140017620.

Yiu, Joseph *The Definitive Guide to the ARM Cortex-M0*; 2nd Edition; 2011, Newnes; ISBN 978-0123854773.

Yiu, Joseph *The Definitive Guide to the ARM Cortex-M3*, 2nd Edition, 2009, Newnes, ISBN 185617963X.

Zhang, Y. (2009). "Remote-sensing Image Classification Based on an Improved Probabilistic Neural Network". Sensors. 9 (9): 7516–7539.doi:10.3390/s90907516. PM 3290485. PMID 22400006.

Resources

- Java Virtual Machine Specification, http:// java.sun.com/docs/books/vmspec/
- NASA Systems Engineering Handbook, NASA SP-2007-6105. Avail: https://ntrs.nasa.gov/archive/nasa/casi.ntrs.nasa.gov/20080008301.pdf
- https://www.arduino.cc/
- https://www.beowulf.org/
- Wikipedia, various

Selected documents available from www.ARM.com:

Cortex-M3 Technical Reference Manual, 2006, ARM Ltd. ARM DDI 0337E.

ARMv6-M Architecture Reference Manual, 2010, ARM Ltd. ARM DDI 0419C.

ARM Architecture Reference Manual, 2005, ARM Ltd, ARM DDI 01001.

"ARM Extends Cortex Family with First Processor Optimized for FPGA", ARM press release, March 19, 2007.

Cortex-A5 Specification Summary.

Cortex-A7 Specification Summary.

Cortex-A8 Specification Summary.

Cortex-A9 Specification Summary.

Cortex-A15 Specification Summary.

Cortex-R4 Specification Summary.

Cortex-R5 Specification Summary.

Cortex-R5 & Cortex-R7 Press Release January 31, 2011.

Cortex-R7 Specification Summary.

Cortex-M0 Specification Summary.

Cortex-M0 Instruction Set.

Cortex-M1 Specification Summary.

Cortex-M3 Specification Summary.

Cortex-M4 Specification Summary.

If you enjoyed this book, you might also be interested in some of these.

Stakem, Patrick H. *16-bit Microprocessors, History and Architecture*, 2013 PRRB Publishing, ISBN-1520210922.

Stakem, Patrick H. *4- and 8-bit Microprocessors, Architecture and History*, 2013, PRRB Publishing, ISBN-152021572X,

Stakem, Patrick H. *Apollo's Computers,* 2014, PRRB Publishing, ISBN-1520215800.

Stakem, Patrick H. *The Architecture and Applications of the ARM Microprocessors,* 2013, PRRB Publishing, ISBN-1520215843.

Stakem, Patrick H. *Earth Rovers: for Exploration and Environmental Monitoring,* 2014, PRRB Publishing, ISBN-152021586X.

Stakem, Patrick H. *Embedded Computer Systems, Volume 1, Introduction and Architecture*, 2013, PRRB Publishing, ISBN-1520215959.

Stakem, Patrick H. *The History of Spacecraft Computers from the V-2 to the Space Station*, 2013, PRRB Publishing, ISBN-1520216181.

Stakem, Patrick H. *Floating Point Computation*, 2013, PRRB Publishing, ISBN-152021619X.

Stakem, Patrick H. *Architecture of Massively Parallel Microprocessor Systems*, 2011, PRRB Publishing, ISBN-1520250061.

Stakem, Patrick H. *Multicore Computer Architecture,* 2014, PRRB Publishing, ISBN-1520241372.

Stakem, Patrick H. *Personal Robots*, 2014, PRRB Publishing, ISBN-1520216254.

Stakem, Patrick H. *RISC Microprocessors, History and Overview,* 2013, PRRB Publishing, ISBN-1520216289.

Stakem, Patrick H. *Robots and Telerobots in Space Applications,* 2011, PRRB Publishing, ISBN-1520210361.

Stakem, Patrick H. *The Saturn Rocket and the Pegasus Missions, 1965,* 2013, PRRB Publishing, ISBN-1520209916.

Stakem, Patrick H. *Visiting the NASA Centers, and Locations of Historic Rockets & Spacecraft,* 2017, PRRB Publishing, ISBN-1549651205.

Stakem, Patrick H. *Microprocessors in Space*, 2011, PRRB Publishing, ISBN-1520216343.

Stakem, Patrick H. Computer *Virtualization and the Cloud*, 2013, PRRB Publishing, ISBN-152021636X.

Stakem, Patrick H. *What's the Worst That Could Happen? Bad Assumptions, Ignorance, Failures and Screw-ups in Engineering Projects, 2014,* PRRB Publishing, ISBN-1520207166.

Stakem, Patrick H. *Computer Architecture & Programming of the Intel x86 Family, 2013,* PRRB Publishing, ISBN-1520263724.

Stakem, Patrick H. *The Hardware and Software Architecture of the Transputer,* 2011,PRRB Publishing, ISBN-152020681X.

Stakem, Patrick H. *Mainframes, Computing on Big Iron,* 2015, PRRB Publishing, ISBN- 1520216459.

Stakem, Patrick H. *Spacecraft Control Centers*, 2015, PRRB Publishing, ISBN-1520200617.

Stakem, Patrick H. *Embedded in Space,* 2015, PRRB Publishing, ISBN-1520215916.

Stakem, Patrick H. *A Practitioner's Guide to RISC Microprocessor Architecture,* Wiley-Interscience, 1996, ISBN 0471130184.

Stakem, Patrick H. *Cubesat Engineeering,* PRRB Publishing, 2017, ISBN-1520754019.

Stakem, Patrick H. *Cubesat Operations,* PRRB Publishing, 2017, ISBN-152076717X.

Stakem, Patrick H. *Interplanetary Cubesats,* PRRB Publishing, 2017, ISBN-1520766173 .

Stakem, Patrick H. Cubesat Constellations, Clusters, and Swarms, Stakem, PRRB Publishing, 2017, ISBN-1520767544.

Stakem, Patrick H. *Graphics Processing Units, an overview,* 2017, PRRB Publishing, ISBN-1520879695.

Stakem, Patrick H. *Intel Embedded and the Arduino-101, 2017,* PRRB Publishing, ISBN-1520879296.

Stakem, Patrick H. *Orbital Debris, the problem and the mitigation,* 2018, PRRB Publishing, ISBN-*1980466483.*

Stakem, Patrick H. *Manufacturing in Space,* 2018, PRRB Publishing, ISBN-1977076041.

Stakem, Patrick H. *NASA's Ships and Planes,* 2018, PRRB Publishing, ISBN-1977076823.

Stakem, Patrick H. *Space Tourism,* 2018, PRRB Publishing, ISBN-1977073506.

Stakem, Patrick H. *STEM – Data Storage and Communications*, 2018, PRRB Publishing, ISBN-1977073115.

Stakem, Patrick H. *In-Space Robotic Repair and Servicing*, 2018, PRRB Publishing, ISBN-1980478236.

Stakem, Patrick H. *Introducing Astronomy in the pre-K to 12 Curricula, A Resource Guide for Educators*, 2017, PRRB Publishing, ISBN-198104065X.
Also available in a Brazilian Portuguese edition, ISBN-1983106127.

Stakem, Patrick H. *Deep Space Gateways, the Moon and Beyond*, 2017, PRRB Publishing, ISBN-1973465701.

Stakem, Patrick H. *Exploration of the Gas Giants, Space Missions to Jupiter, Saturn, Uranus, and Neptune*, PRRB Publishing, 2018, ISBN-9781717814500.

Stakem, Patrick H. *Crewed Spacecraft*, 2017, PRRB Publishing, ISBN-1549992406.

Stakem, Patrick H. *Rocketplanes to Space*, 2017, PRRB Publishing, ISBN-1549992589.

Stakem, Patrick H. *Crewed Space Stations,* 2017, PRRB Publishing, ISBN-1549992228.

Stakem, Patrick H. *Enviro-bots for STEM: Using Robotics in the pre-K to 12 Curricula, A Resource Guide for Educators,* 2017, PRRB Publishing, ISBN-1549656619.

Stakem, Patrick H. *STEM-Sat, Using Cubesats in the pre-K to 12 Curricula, A Resource Guide for Educators*, 2017, ISBN-1549656376.

Stakem, Patrick H. *Lunar Orbital Platform-Gateway*, 2018, PRRB

Publishing, ISBN-1980498628.

Stakem, Patrick H. Embedded GPU's, 2018, PRRB Publishing, ISBN- 1980476497.

Stakem, Patrick H. Mobile Cloud Robotics, 2018, PRRB Publishing, ISBN- 1980488088

Stakem, Patrick H. *Extreme Environment Embedded Systems,* 2017, PRRB Publishing, ISBN-1520215967.

Stakem, Patrick H. *What's the Worst, Volume-2*, 2018, ISBN-1981005579.

Stakem, Patrick H., *Spaceports*, 2018, ISBN-1981022287.

Stakem, Patrick H., *Space Launch Vehicles*, 2018, ISBN-1983071773.

Stakem, Patrick H. *Mars*, 2018, ISBN-1983116902.

Stakem, Patrick H. *X-86, 40th Anniversary ed*, 2018, ISBN-1983189405.

Stakem, Patrick H. *Lunar Orbital Platform-Gateway*, 2018, PRRB Publishing, ISBN-1980498628.

Stakem, Patrick H. *Space Weather*, 2018, ISBN-1723904023.

Stakem, Patrick H. *STEM-Engineering Process*, 2017, ISBN-1983196517.

Stakem, Patrick H. *Space Telescopes,* 2018, PRRB Publishing, ISBN-1728728568.

Stakem, Patrick H. *Exoplanets*, 2018, PRRB Publishing, ISBN-9781731385055.

71

Stakem, Patrick H. *Planetary Defense*, 2018, PRRB Publishing, ISBN-9781731001207.

Patrick H. Stakem *Exploration of the Asteroid Belt*, 2018, PRRB Publishing, ISBN - 1731049846.

Patrick H. Stakem *Terraforming*, 2018, PRRB Publishing, ISBN-1790308100.

Patrick H. Stakem, *Martian Railroad,* 2019, PRRB Publishing, ISBN-1794488243.

Patrick H. Stakem, *Exoplanets,* 2019, PRRB Publishing, ISBN-1731385056.

Patrick H. Stakem, *Exploiting the Moon,* 2019, PRRB Publishing, ISBN-1091057850.

Patrick H. Stakem, *RISC-V, an Open Source Solution for Space Flight Computers,* 2019, PRRB Publishing, ISBN-1796434388.

Patrick H. Stakem, *Arm in Space*, 2019, PRRB Publishing, ISBN-9781099789137.

Patrick H. Stakem, *Extraterrestrial Life*, 2019, PRRB Publishing, ISBN-978-1072072188.

Patrick H. Stakem, *Space Command*, 2019, PRRB Publishing, ISBN-978-*1693005398.*

AGRADECIMIENTOS

Quisiera expresar mi gratitud a todos los que han apoyado este libro y a los aficionados a la programación en ZX Spectrum y BASIC, quienes apoyaron esta idea desde el principio.

Me gustaría agradecer a mi compañera Gabrielle por ayudarme a comprobar parte del código de este libro.

Gracias a mis padres por comprarme el ZX Spectrum como regalo de navidad en los años 80.

Gracias a Richard Langford por el uso de su imagen gráfica de 48k Spectrum.

Gracias a la gran comunidad retro que ayuda a difundir el mensaje.

Gracias a Sir Clive Sinclair por crear el Sinclair ZX Spectrum.

AGRADECIMIENTOS ESPECIALES

A Gabby y Pippin por todas las largas noches

Publicado por primera vez en 2015 por Gazzapper Press

http://www.gazzapper.com

Portada diseñada por Gary Plowman

Publicado por Gazzapper Press

Derechos de autor © 2015 Gary Plowman

Todos los derechos reservados.

ISBN-10: 0993474446
ISBN-13: 978-0993474446 (Gazzapper Press)

CLUB DE PROGRAMACION DE JUEGOS DE ZX SPECTRUM

Veinte juegos para teclear, aprender de ellos, y ampliarlos

Gary Plowman

Índice

TIC TAC TOE.. 19

ZX BREAKOUT... 27

SNAKE BITE.. 34

FLAPPY BIRD.. 41

THE NUMBERS GAME.. 47

BATTLESHIP WAR.. 53

CODEBREAK.. 60

ASTRAL INVADERS... 64

COLOUR STACKS.. 69

ANGRY CHICKY.. 73

ALLOTMENT WARS.. 78

RETRO HUNTER.. 84

SNOWBALL SHOOTOUT.. 89

TETRIX.. 95

TYPE INVADERS... 102

MINIPONG... 106

TAKEAWAY TED... 109

C5 SOLAR RACE.. 114

PENALTY SHOOTOUT.. 118

BILLY BOB'S GOLD.. 121

ANEXO A – Mapa de caracteres.. 127

ACERCA DEL AUTOR 131

INTRODUCCIÓN

Antes de empezar, vamos a aclarar el propósito de este libro. Este no pretende ser un libro de referencia sobre los entresijos del lenguaje Sinclair BASIC. Este es un libro para facilitar el aprendizaje de Sinclair BASIC, mientras escribimos código para crear diversos juegos. Adicionalmente, disfrutarás de algunos juegos de la "vieja escuela" gracias a tu propio esfuerzo. A medida que avancemos por el libro, haremos menos explicaciones para no aburrirnos. Hay diversos tipos de juegos en este libro, por lo que espero que haya algo de interés para todos.

Tal vez quieras contar a las generaciones más jóvenes sobre los días de gloria de la primera etapa de la microcomputación. O tal vez quieras ofrecer actividades fáciles de aprender en el club de código de tu localidad, que todos puedan realizar sin necesidad de ser un experto o un sapientín. O quizás sólo seas fan de ZX y te has comprado un ZX Spectrum Bluetooth. De cualquier manera, esperamos que te diviertas mientras aprendes y practicas con este libro.

Cuando era adolescente aprendí sobre programación en BASIC. La experiencia me abrió puertas a muchas posibilidades y me ayudó a sentir pasión por la computación y la programación en general. Hoy en día, me dedico a la programación de escritorio, web y móvil para desarrollar juegos, aplicaciones de negocios y startups en Internet. Todo el mundo tiene que empezar en algún lugar y nunca es demasiado tarde o muy pronto para aprender a programar.

Entonces ¿por qué Sinclair BASIC?

El lenguaje Sinclair BASIC es una de las puertas de entrada a la programación profesional. Con él comenzaron muchos programadores exitosos, británicos y europeos, antes de pasar a programar juegos y herramientas increíbles durante la década de 1980. Todo esto se hizo con menos de 48k de RAM. Algunos ejemplos son RARE (también conocido como Ultimate Play the Game o ACG), The Oliver Twins (Serie Dizzy), Codemasters y muchos más.

BASIC significa "Beginners All Purpose Symbolic Instruction Code" (código de instrucción simbólica de todo propósito para principiantes) y es perfecto para principiantes. Es amigable y divertido. Sus comandos son lógicos y llamados de acuerdo la función que realizan.

Con Sinclair BASIC podrás aprender lógica, cómo tomar decisiones y cómo estructurar su código, pero sólo para conceptos simples. También es de ayuda para habilidades matemáticas básicas (sin necesidad de ser un Gurú para aprender a utilizarlo).

ROM BASIC (Read Only Memory o memoria de sólo lectura) es el sistema operativo de la máquina Sinclair. Está configurado de manera tal que no permite el ingreso de código ilegal. Cada línea es validada por la ROM, por lo que después de ingresar una línea podrás escuchar un pitido que indica que la línea ha sido introducida correctamente. Si la línea es incorrecta, se podrá escuchar un sonido de tonalidad inferior y el sistema pedirá la corrección del código incorrecto.

Quiero extender una nota de agradecimiento especial a los chicos de Sinclair, especialmente a Steve Vickers y al resto de los integrantes de Nine Tiles Ltd. por la creación de Sinclair BASIC.

¿Qué necesitamos antes de empezar?

Cualquiera de las siguientes configuraciones está bien para empezar:

a) ZX Spectrum: por ejemplo ZX Spectrum 16k, 48k, 48K+, 128K o cualquier otro modelo.

B) Un ordenador que pueda ejecutar un emulador: Ejemplo de algunos emuladores para varias plataformas

Windows: ZX Spin, Spectaculator, Speccy, entre otros

Mac OS: Fuse

Linux/Unix: Fuse

iOS/Android: Spectaculator, Fuse, Speccy, Marvin

Chrome/FF: Hay un par de emuladores en línea que funcionan desde un navegador. Podrás encontrarlos si buscas un poco en Google, pero aquí hay dos ejemplos que seguramente funcionarán en tu navegador.

http://jsspeccy.zxdemo.org

http://torinak.com/qaop

C) Otra buena opción es el nuevo Recreated ZX Spectrum (Bluetooth) que funciona en Android e iOS.

Para principiantes con el ZX Spectrum, puedo sugerir programación en **modo 128k**, pues permite comandos mecanografiados y no requiere la combinación de teclas requerida por el modo 48k. Sin embargo, si estás listo para el desafío o quieres revivir momentos de nostalgia, entonces lo tuyo será el modo 48k o 16k.

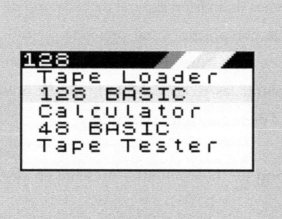

Inicio rápido

Si quieres empezar escribir código ahora mismo y tienes alguna de las opciones mencionadas anteriormente, puedes pasar por alto esta sección y comenzar a programar cualquiera de los juegos de inmediato.

Comandos básicos

Algunos de los comandos más comunes que vamos a utilizar son PRINT, IF, GOTO, GO SUB, DIM y LET. Sólo veremos una visión general de cada uno de ellos, ya que este es un libro para el aprendizaje por práctica y no pretende ser utilizado como manual. Encontrar tantos tecnicismos a la hora de leer puede ser aburrido. Los mejor es comenzar a presionar las abultadas teclas del Spectrum 48k o escuchar los tonos de plástico del Spectrum 128k o de tu emulador preferido.

Este es el ejemplo obligatorio de "hola mundo", presente en casi todos los libros de programación.

Presiona Enter al final de la línea para guardarlo en la memoria, luego escribe RUN y pulsa Enter de nuevo para ejecutarlo.

El desglose de código del ejemplo anterior es:

10	=	Numeración de líneas (secuencia del programa)
PRINT	=	Impresión en la pantalla (¡fácil!)
AT y,x	=	Dictar al programa las coordenadas para PRINT (IMPRIMIR) en donde 'y' es el eje vertical y 'x' horizontal
;	=	Permite una nueva sub-función o que el texto se imprima
"Hello World"	=	Contenido del texto

PRINT ingresará texto o caracteres gráficos especiales (es decir, UDG) en la pantalla y en la posición que especifique. La pantalla de ZX Spectrum es de 32 columnas de caracteres de ancho (0 a 31) por 22 líneas de largo (0 a 21). La parte AT (operando) del comando le dicta que coloque los elementos en Y (línea), X (Columna). Hay 2 líneas adicionales, pero estas no se utilizan con el comando PRINT estándar.

Las siguientes sub-funciones funcionarán en línea con el comando PRINT:

INK <0-7>	Establece el color de primer plano para el bolígrafo, que imprime todo el texto y los gráficos
PAPER <0-7>	Establece el color del fondo de papel de la pantalla principal
INVERSE <1 o 0>	Imprime e invierte la configuración actual de INK y PAPER
PAPEROVER <1 o 0>	Activa/desactiva la sobreimpresión en la pantalla
FLASH <1 o 0>	El flash alternará repetidamente entre los colores actuales e invertidos
BRIGHT <1 o 0 o 8>	Versiones más brillantes de los colores 1 - 6 (para INK y PAPER). 8 es transparente
TAB #	Mueve horizontalmente de izquierda a derecha # espacios

Ejemplo: PRINT INK 2; AT 10,10;"Test"; TAB 16;PAPER 1;INK 7;FLASH 1;"Print"
Como puedes ver, se puede tener casi cualquier combinación de estos comandos en una sentencia PRINT.

Numeración de líneas

Dejar un espacio adecuado en la numeración de líneas de código, es una buena práctica para poder ingresar comandos adicionales posteriormente. Sugiero que para tus programas dejes al menos unos 10 espacios. Así verás algo como línea 10, luego línea 20 y así sucesivamente. Sinclair BASIC puede tener un máximo de 9999 líneas, pero las líneas pueden contener varias sentencias cuando están separadas por dos puntos ":", por lo que los comandos pueden ejecutarse en decenas de miles.

Modo 128k y Línea de números

El modo 128k Spectrum tiene otra característica muy útil para principiantes. Si el programa no tiene una sección y no has generado suficiente espacio para los comandos, puedes ejecutar RENUMBER y la numeración de líneas del programa se reorganizará. Hay limitaciones al respecto, pero no debemos preocuparnos por ello en un principio.

UDG (User Defined Graphics o Gráficos definidos por el usuario)

¡Aprenderás cómo hacer tus propios gráficos con facilidad! Así podrás volver a algunos de los juegos de este libro y agregar tus propios gráficos para mejorarlos y ampliarlos.

Código de máquina

A los efectos de este libro, el código de máquina puede ser un poco difícil de entender. Así que no hablaremos de ello. Sin embargo, inscríbete en nuestras alertas en Gazzapper.com, pues quizás publiquemos versiones actualizadas de algunos de los juegos, con algunas rutinas de código de máquina.

¿Qué es una "Lista type-in"?

En los primeros días de la microcomputación, las revistas publicaban 'listas' o 'listas type-in' para que los aficionados (codificadores/programadores) pudieran ingresar código desde la comodidad de sus habitaciones. Algunas listas contenían errores que causaban frustración en los usuarios y, por lo tanto, generaban ira hacia el autor. Si no era posible arreglar los bugs, el usuario quedaba atascado en un código que no funcionaba, después de pasar horas trabajando en él.

Bien, puedo decir que he escrito y comprobado todas las listas. Cualquier problema puede ser resuelto a través del nuevo grupo de Facebook que he creado, llamado **ZX Spectrum Code Club.** O si ya eres miembro de un grupo de ZX Spectrum, simplemente publica tus preguntas allí (si sus reglas lo permiten).

Las listas fueron escritas de forma que permitan sacar el máximo provecho de las limitaciones de velocidad de Sinclair BASIC (dentro de lo estimado), para que los juegos sean divertidos y aptos para jugar. La estructura está hecha para ser fácil de seguir y, aunque no es perfecta, permitirá al usuario saber lo que sucede dentro de cada juego. La estructura de los juegos es bastante similar, así que podrás familiarizarte con ellos y, por lo tanto, es una plantilla simple que podrás usar en tus propias creaciones.

Una gran característica de Sinclair BASIC es que la ROM valida la mayoría del código antes de aceptar las sentencias. En caso de que no lo hayas leído antes, ROM significa Memoria de Sólo Lectura y contiene el sistema operativo y varias rutinas requeridas por BASIC.

Aunque las sentencias REM no son necesarias para el funcionamiento de los programas, es bueno mencionarlas, ya que mientras más código agregues a un programa, más comentarios se necesitan, especialmente para que el usuario se dirija a cada edición o extensión del código posteriormente. También pueden ser útiles como divisores visuales entre las secciones de tu programa, para que sea más fácil de leer.

Sinclair BASIC no es el lenguaje de programación más rápido, pero si uno de los más divertidos y fáciles de aprender. Sin entrar en demasiados detalles técnicos, un usuario puede acelerar cualquiera de los emuladores de Spectrum en las opciones, aumentando la velocidad de ejecución del emulador desde la velocidad estándar de 3.54MHz a la velocidad x2 o superior.

Mapeo del teclado del emulador

Cuando se utiliza un emulador sobre una máquina Spectrum, hay algunas complejidades que deben señalarse en relación con la asignación de las teclas. Más abajose muestra un diseño real de 48k Spectrum.

Seleccionar símbolos como comillas y *, entre otros, puede ser diferente en tu teclado de tu PC o MAC, que en el del emulador. Este puede ser el caso de algunos teclados y emuladores. Puedes ver que ciertos símbolos serán diferentes en tu teclado.

Equivalentes de teclado estándar para los emuladores Sinclair

A continuación se muestra una lista que muestra cómo algunas de las asignaciones de teclado pueden diferir. Ten en cuenta que algunos emuladores pueden utilizar Alt en lugar de Ctrl para algunas de estas asignaciones.

* (asterisco)	=	Ctrl + B	; (punto y coma) =		Alt Gr + O
(	=	Ctrl + 8	: (dos puntos)	=	Alt + Gr
)	=	Ctrl + 9	Suprimir	=	Shift + 0 (cero)
" (comillas)	=	Ctrl + P	Modo gráfico	=	Shift + 9
. (punto)	=	Alt Gr + M	Cerrar / Quitar	=	Shift + Espacio
, (coma)	=	Alt Gr + N	Modo Extendido =		Shift + Ctrl

Nota: Alt Gr es la tecla Alt ubicada a la derecha de la barra espaciadora

Si te atascas en cualquier problema, envía tu consulta a uno de los muchos grupos de ZX Spectrum en Facebook.

Guardando tus Type-Ins

Esto es relativamente sencillo para usuarios de emuladores: sólo tienes que guardar un archivo snapshot (.sna). Los usuarios de la máquina "real", necesitaréis una grabadora de cintas de la vieja escuela y un cassette en blanco C15, C30, C60 o C90. Para guardar el type-in, debes pulsar "Play & Record" en tu reproductor de cintas (con micrófono y auriculares conectados) y utiliza SAVE "<Typein Name>" LINE 10.

Usar un MicroDrive

Guardar en un MicroDrive o en un MicroDrive emulado puede hacerse de la siguiente manera:

SAVE *"m";1;"My Program"

A continuación, puedes verificar el guardado utilizando:

VERIFY *"m";1;"My Program"

Para eliminar un programa sólo tienes que utilizar:

ERASE "m";1;"My Program"

Para cargar un programa:

LOAD *"m";1;"My Program"

Para ver el contenido (catálogo) de un disco MicroDrive:

CAT 1 o Cat

 (Nota: CAT también se utiliza con el modelo 128k + 3)

Pueden añadirse LOAD * y SAVE * en MicroDrive con el sufijo CODE, SCREEN $ y LINE #, similar a los comandos LOAD y SAVE estándar.

Fundamentos del Game Loop

El Game Loop es la parte del juego donde ocurre toda la acción y que se ejecuta repetidamente hasta que el juego ha terminado. Sigue una cierta estructura o secuencia de eventos. Esta estructura no está escrita en piedra, pero a continuación te mostraré un ejemplo sencillo de cómo un Game Loop se ajusta al código.

---- Configuración: UDG Gráfico (también conocido como Sprites) o carga de datos

---- Inicializar: Variables clave, cadenas y arrays

---- Menú / Pantalla de inicio para el juego

    ---- Game Loop:

    ---- Proceso Input / pulsaciones de teclas

    ---- Actualización de posiciones / Actualizaciones de IA, etc.

    ---- Dibujar / Imprimir elementos de la pantalla

    ---- Repetir Loop

---- Fin / Salir de juego

He utilizado este tipo de estructura para la mayoría de los juegos de este libro. Espero que el formato te ayude a entender lo que hace un Game Loop y cómo se debe utilizar.

Sugerencia: Presionar 'Shift' y 'Espacio', te hará salir (BREAK / QUIT) de un programa en ejecución.

Cómo usar este libro

Puedes programar o copiar estas listas en cualquier orden que desees. Quizás algunos comandos o conceptos más nuevos no estén explicados con el detalle con el que se pudieron exponer en una lista anterior, pero eso está bien. Llegarás allí eventualmente. Recuerda que esto es por diversión, así que si un juego determinado no es de tu interés, no dudes en saltarlo.

Ten en cuenta esta regla muy útil del carácter de espacio en el libro impreso: cada 12 caracteres son 3 cm aproximadamente.

Escanea, copia, imprime o simplemente vuelve a consultar para calcular espacios en las listas de código, si es necesario. También puedes hacer tu propio juego. Los listados son monoespaciados, por lo que serán fáciles de usar.

Algunos consejos prácticos al escribir código ...

1) Para acelerar la escritura de datos, es recomendable pedir a alguien que te dicte la lista de código, línea por línea.

2) Otro método consiste en utilizar una regla u otro libro para ocultar las líneas que aún no has escrito.

3) ¡Comprueba siempre que el número de línea sea correcto! Muchos cometen errores tipográficos al escribir números.

Así que sin más demoras, ¡empecemos a escribir nuestros juegos!

TIC TAC TOE
O
NOUGHTS AND CROSSES

Empecemos con uno sencillo. Tic Tac Toe, o Noughts and Crosses, es un juego sencillo y universal. La mayoría de las personas lo ha jugado al menos una vez en la vida, usando lápiz y papel. Muchos libros del colegio estaban llenos de 'x' y 'o'.

Jugadores: 2

Reglas: El jugador 1 intenta completar una fila de 'X' y el jugador 2 intenta completar una fila de 'O'.

Controles: Las teclas del 1 al 9 seleccionarán la posición en la cuadrícula. Puedes ver la cuadrícula de posiciones a continuación.

1 2 3

4 5 6

7 8 9

```
  10 REM **********ZX CODE CLUB***************
  15 REM * Tic-Tac-Toe or Noughts and Crosses *
  20 REM ********** Gary Plowman *************
  30 INK 7: PAPER 6: BORDER 7: CLS : LET ply=1: LET win=0: DIM
a(9,2): LET sq=0
  40 GO SUB 90
  50 GO TO 300
  60 REM ********** DRAW BOARD
  90 PRINT AT 2,10; INK 1;"Tic Tac Toe"
 110 PLOT INK 5;100,40: DRAW INK 5;0,100
```

```
 120 PLOT INK 5;150,40: DRAW INK 5;0,100
 130 PLOT INK 5;65,70: DRAW INK 5;120,0
 140 PLOT INK 5;65,110: DRAW INK 5;120,0
 160 REM State 1=player 1, 2=Player 2
 175 INK 5: PLOT 50,170: DRAW -40,-40: PLOT 10,170: DRAW 40,-
40
 180 CIRCLE INK 4;220,150,20
 190 PRINT ; INK 0; PAPER 3;AT 14,0;"1 2 3";AT 15,0;"4 5 6";AT
16,0;"7 8 9"
 210 RETURN
 300 REM ******* Test Press
 310 PRINT AT 18,1; INK 7; PAPER 6-ply;"PLAYER ";ply;" Choose
Square 1 - 9"
 320 LET i$=INKEY$()
 330 IF i$>="1" AND i$<="9" THEN LET square=VAL i$: GO SUB
1000
 340 IF i$="" THEN GOTO 320
 350 GO SUB 2000: REM ****** Test for Winning Conditions :)
 355 IF sq=9 THEN LET win=-1
 360 IF win>0 THEN PRINT AT 18,1;"PLAYER ";win;" has WON!":
BEEP .4,3: BEEP 2,10: GO TO 10
 370 IF win<0 THEN PRINT AT 18,1;"GAME DRAWN - RESTARTING":
BEEP .4,3: BEEP 2,10: GO TO 10
 400 GO TO 300
1000 REM ******* Check squares
1010 IF a(square,1)=1 OR a(square,2)=1 THEN PRINT AT 18,1; INK
3;"Square Taken Already": BEEP .3,1: GO TO 1050
1020 LET a(square,ply)=1: LET ply=ply+1: LET sq=sq+1
1025 PRINT AT 18,1; INK 4;"Good move!": BEEP .4,12
1030 IF ply=3 THEN LET ply=1
1040 GO SUB 3000: REM ******* Draw Move
1050 PRINT AT 18,1;"                              "
1090 RETURN
2000 REM ***** WINNING CONDITIONS CHECK
2010 FOR n=1 TO 2
2020 IF a(1,n)=1 AND a(2,n)=1 AND a(3,n)=1 THEN LET win=n
```

```
2030 IF a(1,n)=1 AND a(4,n)=1 AND a(7,n)=1 THEN LET win=n
2040 IF a(2,n)=1 AND a(5,n)=1 AND a(8,n)=1 THEN LET win=n
2050 IF a(3,n)=1 AND a(6,n)=1 AND a(9,n)=1 THEN LET win=n
2060 IF a(3,n)=1 AND a(5,n)=1 AND a(7,n)=1 THEN LET win=n
2070 IF a(1,n)=1 AND a(5,n)=1 AND a(9,n)=1 THEN LET win=n
2080 IF a(4,n)=1 AND a(5,n)=1 AND a(6,n)=1 THEN LET win=n
2090 IF a(7,n)=1 AND a(8,n)=1 AND a(9,n)=1 THEN LET win=n
2100 NEXT n
2110 RETURN
3000 REM ******* DRAW MOVE
3010 LET posx=80: LET posy=130: REM ***** where to draw
3020 IF square=1 THEN LET posx=80: LET posy=130
3030 IF square=2 THEN LET posx=130: LET posy=130
3040 IF square=3 THEN LET posx=180: LET posy=130
3050 IF square=4 THEN LET posx=80: LET posy=100
3060 IF square=5 THEN LET posx=130: LET posy=100
3070 IF square=6 THEN LET posx=180: LET posy=100
3080 IF square=7 THEN LET posx=80: LET posy=70
3090 IF square=8 THEN LET posx=130: LET posy=70
3100 IF square=9 THEN LET posx=180: LET posy=70
3300 IF ply=1 THEN CIRCLE INK 4;posx-10,posy-10,10
3310 IF ply=2 THEN INK 5: PLOT posx,posy: DRAW -20,-20: PLOT
posx-20,posy: DRAW 20,-20
3350 RETURN
```

¡Enhorabuena!
¡Lo has logrado!

Ahora que has completado tu primer juego, puedes comenzar a jugarlo. Para ejecutar un programa en BASIC, escribe RUN en el indicador y luego presiona la tecla Enter.

Después de jugar

No vamos a repasar todas las líneas, sólo las cosas más importantes o aquellas que creo que podrían ser más difíciles de entender.

Entonces, ¿qué significa todo esto? Las líneas de 10 a 20 son sólo para mostrar. El comando REM es para agregar cualquier comentario sobre el código.

```
10 REM ******************************************
15 REM * Tic-Tac-Toe or Noughts and Crosses *
20 REM ********** Gary Plowman ************
```

La línea 30 configura la pantalla del juego. El comando INK es el color del bolígrafo, PAPER es el área de la pantalla principal y BORDER es la zona fuera del área de la pantalla principal. El área de la frontera (BORDER) casi no se usa y no entra en el rango de los comandos PLOT o PRINT, pero se puede hacer flash para indicar un golpe o marcar un punto.

```
30 INK 7: PAPER 6: BORDER 7: CLS : LET ply=1: LET win=0: DIM
a(9,2): LET sq=0
```

Lo siguiente en esa línea es CLS. Esto significa 'borrar la pantalla' (Clear The Screen) y, sin esto, el comando PAPER no podría cambiar el área de la pantalla de color. Después de esto, el comando LET se utiliza para configurar variables. Las variables almacenan los valores que se utilizarán o cambiarán posteriormente en el código.

Arrays y Arrays Multidimensionales

Esta parte no es difícil. Sin embargo, no te preocupes si aún no consigues Arrays. Los Arrays son difíciles al principio y es mejor pensar en ellos como listas de valores.

La última parte de la línea 30 es el comando DIM a(9,2) (array dimensional). Este es un array de variables y funciona como una lista u hoja de cálculo en orden numérico. Si no lo entiendes tal vez esto lo explicará mejor.

La primera dimensión puede ser pensada como **columna 1** que contiene 9 filas de datos. La segunda parte se refiere a la **columna 2** con un conjunto diferente de 9 filas de datos.

```
DIM a(9,2) - 9 rows down with 2 columns

Column 1                Column 2
LET a(1,1)=1            LET a(1,2)=1    - Row 1
...                     ...
LET a(9,1)=9            LET a(9,2)=9    - Row 9
```

Los comandos anteriores almacenarán valores en diferentes secciones del array. Se producirá un error si intentas superar los límites del array, establecidos en la sentencia DIM. Los arrays en Sinclair BASIC siempre comienzan desde 1 y no desde 0 (cero).

Explicación de GO SUB

El comando GO SUB significa Go Subroutine. GO SUB permitirá que un programa salte a la otra parte del código, basado en el número de líneas proporcionado, y luego puede volver a la posición anterior si encuentra una sentencia RETURN. Esto es muy útil para dividir un programa BASIC en secciones lógicas. Es muy útil contar con un GO SUB para cualquier extensión de código que quieras agregar a cualquiera de los juegos. Cada problema importante que encuentres puede separarse como una rutina GO SUB, lo que te ayudará a realizar un seguimiento de tu programa.

Resumen del programa restante

Las líneas 90 a 210 dibujan el contenido de la pantalla del juego.

```
 90 PRINT AT 2,10; INK 1;"Tic Tac Toe"
110 PLOT INK 5;100,40: DRAW INK 5;0,100
120 PLOT INK 5;150,40: DRAW INK 5;0,100
```

```
130 PLOT INK 5;65,70: DRAW INK 5;120,0
140 PLOT INK 5;65,110: DRAW INK 5;120,0
160 REM State 1=player 1, 2=Player 2
175 INK 5: PLOT 50,170: DRAW -40,-40: PLOT 10,170: DRAW 40,-
40
180 CIRCLE INK 4;220,150,20
190 PRINT ; INK 0; PAPER 3;AT 14,0;"1 2 3";AT 15,0;"4 5 6";AT
16,0;"7 8 9"
210 RETURN
```

Las líneas 110 a 140 con PLOT, crean los puntos de partida para dibujar. Estas líneas dibujan el # de cuadrículas para el juego. El comando PLOT coloca el bolígrafo en la pantalla (haciendo un punto). A continuación, el comando DRAW crea una línea o un arco.

Las líneas 175 a 190 dibujarán los símbolos X y O a los lados de la cuadrícula y también imprimirán la cuadrícula para los controles del jugador.

Las líneas 300 a 400 ejecutarán el Game Loop principal, que es bastante corto en este juego.

```
300 REM ******* Test Press
310 PRINT AT 18,1; INK 7; PAPER 6-ply;"PLAYER ";ply;" Choose
Square 1 - 9"
320 LET i$=INKEY$()
330 IF i$>="1" AND i$<="9" THEN LET square=VAL i$: GO SUB
1000
340 IF i$="" THEN GOTO 320
350 GO SUB 2000: REM ****** Test for Winning Conditions :)
355 IF sq=9 THEN LET win=-1
360 IF win>0 THEN PRINT AT 18,1;"PLAYER ";win;" has WON!":
BEEP .4,3: BEEP 2,10: GO TO 10
370 IF win<0 THEN PRINT AT 18,1;"GAME DRAWN - RESTARTING":
BEEP .4,3: BEEP 2,10: GO TO 10
400 GO TO 300
```

La línea 320 es importante, debido a que capta las pulsaciones de teclas de los jugadores.

La línea 330 comprueba que la tecla pulsada es válida (es decir, entre 1 y 9)

Las líneas 1000 a 1090 comprueban y aseguran que el cuadrado escogido dentro de la cuadrícula no está ocupado.

```
1000 REM ******* Check squares
1010 IF a(square,1)=1 OR a(square,2)=1 THEN PRINT AT 18,1; INK
3;"Square Taken Already": BEEP .3,1: GO TO 1050
1020 LET a(square,ply)=1: LET ply=ply+1 : LET sq=sq+1
1025 PRINT AT 18,1; INK 4;"Good move!": BEEP .4,12
1030 IF ply=3 THEN LET ply=1
1040 GO SUB 3000: REM ******* Draw Move
1050 PRINT AT 18,1;"                         "
1090 RETURN
```

Las líneas 2000 a 2110 comprueban si fueron alcanzadas las condiciones para ganar el juego. Si encuentra un ganador, el programa lo anunciará y el juego se reiniciará.

```
2000 REM ***** WINNING CONDITIONS CHECK
2010 FOR n=1 TO 2
2020 IF a(1,n)=1 AND a(2,n)=1 AND a(3,n)=1 THEN LET win=n
2030 IF a(1,n)=1 AND a(4,n)=1 AND a(7,n)=1 THEN LET win=n
2040 IF a(2,n)=1 AND a(5,n)=1 AND a(8,n)=1 THEN LET win=n
2050 IF a(3,n)=1 AND a(6,n)=1 AND a(9,n)=1 THEN LET win=n
2060 IF a(3,n)=1 AND a(5,n)=1 AND a(7,n)=1 THEN LET win=n
2070 IF a(1,n)=1 AND a(5,n)=1 AND a(9,n)=1 THEN LET win=n
2080 IF a(4,n)=1 AND a(5,n)=1 AND a(6,n)=1 THEN LET win=n
2090 IF a(7,n)=1 AND a(8,n)=1 AND a(9,n)=1 THEN LET win=n
2100 NEXT n
2110 RETURN
```

Las líneas 3000 a 3350 dibujarán una nueva marca en el tablero dependiendo de a quién corresponde el turno.

```
3000 REM ******* DRAW MOVE
3010 LET posx=80: LET posy=130: REM ***** where to draw
3020 IF square=1 THEN LET posx=80: LET posy=130
3030 IF square=2 THEN LET posx=130: LET posy=130
3040 IF square=3 THEN LET posx=180: LET posy=130
3050 IF square=4 THEN LET posx=80: LET posy=100
3060 IF square=5 THEN LET posx=130: LET posy=100
3070 IF square=6 THEN LET posx=180: LET posy=100
3080 IF square=7 THEN LET posx=80: LET posy=70
3090 IF square=8 THEN LET posx=130: LET posy=70
3100 IF square=9 THEN LET posx=180: LET posy=70
3300 IF ply=1 THEN CIRCLE INK 4;posx-10,posy-10,10
3310 IF ply=2 THEN INK 5: PLOT posx,posy: DRAW -20,-20: PLOT
posx-20,posy: DRAW 20,-20
3350 RETURN
```

¡FELICIDADES! Has alcanzado el NIVEL 1

No ha sido muy difícil de entender. Tomando en cuenta que ahora ya tienes algún conocimiento de BASIC, quizás quieras considerar los siguientes ejercicios para ampliar el juego. Si necesitas más tiempo, puedes seguir avanzando y empezar a programar tu próximo juego.

Sugerencias para ampliar el juego (opcional)

1] Crear un cómputo para que el primer jugador en ganar cinco partidas sea el ganador.

2] Añadir partidas de un solo jugador contra el ordenador con algunas IA básicas (Inteligencia artificial)*

3] Dibujar una línea a través de los cuadrados ganadores

Una IA sencilla no es muy difícil de desarrollar.

ZX BREAKOUT

Está basado en Breakout, el juego arcade original de Atari. Mi primera experiencia jugando Breakout fue en un salón de billar cerca de casa. Creo que fue el primer juego arcade a color que jugué, aunque más tarde me sentí engañado. El juego era realmente en blanco y negro. Los colores adicionales se lograron utilizando una superposición de plástico transparente de color. El efecto en pantalla era bastante similar al del 'colour clash' del ZX Spectrum. Sin embargo, su magia funcionó y me enganché. Por cierto, ¿mencioné que Breakout fue creado por los dos fundadores principales de Apple?

Jugadores: 1

Reglas: El jugador debe lanzar la pelota y evitar que caiga más allá de la raqueta.

Elimina 70 puntos en bloques para pasar a la siguiente pantalla.

Controles: z = izquierda, x = derecha, [espacio] = lanzar pelota.

```
 10 REM *********ZX CODE CLUB***************
 15 REM * ZX BREAKOUT by G Plowman 2015      *
 20 REM ********************************
 25 GO SUB 7000
 30 INK 1: PAPER 7: BORDER 4: CLS
 35 LET lives=3
 45 REM ****** Initialising variables
 50 PRINT AT 2,10; INK 7; BRIGHT 1; PAPER 2;"ZX BREAKOUT";
BRIGHT 0; PAPER 7; INK 1;AT  6,0;"Taken from..";AT 8,0;"ZX
Spectrum Games Code Club Book": PAUSE 0
 100 GO SUB 300: REM initialise
 120 GO SUB 500: REM menu
 130 GO SUB 1000: REM main loop for game
```

```
 200 GO TO 30
 300 LET ply=2: LET win=0: DIM a(9,2): DIM d(30): LET lvl=1:
LET posy=30: LET x=10: LET time=0: LET score=0: LET timer=0:
LET mov=11: LET pos=11: LET vx=0: LET vy=0: LET speed=1: LET
ball=0: LET bx=0: LET by=0: LET score2=0
 310 LET b$=" "+CHR$ (147)+CHR$ (145)+" " : LET w$=CHR$
(146)+CHR$ (146)
 400 RETURN
 500 CLS
 510 LET w$=CHR$ (146)
 520 FOR n = 0 TO 31
 530 PRINT INK 2;AT 1,n;w$;AT 21,n;w$
 540 NEXT n
 545 FOR n = 0 TO 20:
 546 PRINT INK 2; AT n,0;w$;AT n,31;w$
 549 NEXT n
 550 RETURN
1000 REM Main Loop
1005 PRINT AT 20,x-2;" ";b$;" "
1010 LET i$=INKEY$(): LET kemp=IN 31
1020 LET timer=timer+1:
1030 IF (i$="z" OR kemp=2) AND x>2 THEN LET x=x-1:
1040 IF (i$="x" OR kemp=1) AND x<29 THEN LET x=x+1
1045 IF i$="z" OR i$="x" OR kemp>0 THEN PRINT AT 20,x-2;"
";b$;" "
1050 IF (i$=CHR$ (32) OR kemp=16) AND ball=0 THEN LET
vx=(RND*1.5)-(RND*1.5): LET vy=-1: LET ball=1: LET bx=x: LET
by=19
1060 IF timer=5 THEN GO SUB 3000
1070 IF ball=1 THEN GO SUB 4000
1080 PRINT AT 0,2;"SCORE:";score;" (Lvl:";lvl;")
Lives:";lives:
2000 GO TO 1010
3000 REM draw blocks
3010 FOR n = 1 TO 20 STEP 2
3020 FOR p = 1 TO 10 STEP 2
```

```
3025 LET ir=RND*4+1
3030 PRINT AT p+2,n+4; INK 0; PAPER ir;"__":
3050 NEXT p
3060 NEXT n
3070 LET timer = 6
3100 RETURN
4000 REM **** BALL MOVE
4005 PRINT AT by,bx;" "
4010 LET bx=bx+vx: LET by=by+vy
4014 LET y$ =SCREEN$ (INT (by),INT (bx))
4015 IF y$="_" THEN LET score = score + 1: BEEP .008,vx+bx:
LET score2=score2+1: LET vy=-vy*speed
4016 IF by>=19 AND ABS (bx-x)<2 THEN LET vx=((RND*2)+1)-
((RND*2)+1): LET vy=-vy*speed: PRINT AT 20,x-2;" ";b$;" "
4020 PRINT AT by,bx; INK 2;CHR$ (144)
4040 IF bx>29 THEN LET vx=-(vx*speed)
4050 IF bx<2 THEN LET vx=-(vx*speed)
4060 IF by>=20 THEN LET ball=0: LET lives=lives-1: BORDER 2:
BEEP 1,0: BORDER 4
4070 IF by<3 THEN LET vy=-(vy*speed)
4080 IF lives=0 THEN GO SUB 5000:
4090 IF score2>=70 THEN GO SUB 6000: REM Next level:
4200 RETURN
5000 REM **** restart
5010 PRINT AT 10,5; FLASH 1; PAPER 6; INK 2;"G A M E   O V E
R"
5030 FOR n =1 TO 200
5050 NEXT n
5100 PRINT AT 12,5;"PRESS KEY TO RESTART"
5110 IF INKEY$="" THEN GO TO 5110
5120 GO TO 30
6000 REM **** NEXT LEVEL
6005 LET lvl=lvl+1: CLS : PRINT AT 10,10; FLASH 1; "L E V E L
";lvl
6010 BEEP 1,13
6020 LET timer=2
```

```
6050 FOR n=1 TO 100
6055 BEEP .001,n/10
6060 NEXT n
6070 LET score2=0
6080 LET ball=0
6100 GO TO 120
7000 REM **** CREATE UDG GRAPHICS!!
7010 FOR n = 0 TO 31
7020 READ graph
7030 POKE USR "a"+n,graph
7050 NEXT n
7060 RETURN
7190 REM *************BALL
7200 DATA BIN 00111100
7210 DATA BIN 01100110
7220 DATA BIN 01011110
7230 DATA BIN 01011110
7240 DATA BIN 01111110
7250 DATA BIN 00111100
7260 DATA BIN 00000000
7270 DATA BIN 00000000
7280 REM *************BAT left side- using full numbers
7300 DATA 252,42,41,2,252,248,0,224
7370 REM *************wall
7400 DATA 231,195,165,24,24,165,195,231
7470 REM *********** BAT right side
7480 DATA 63,84,148,64,63,31,0,7
```

¿Qué hay de nuevo?

La función RND se utiliza para generar un valor Aleatorio entre 0 y 1, que se multiplica por un valor que determina el rango de los valores involucrados. Ejemplo: INT (RND*10) devolverá un valor INTEGER de RND*10, por lo que un valor entre 0 y 9 como comando INT, redondea un número a CERO decimales.

Otras cosas nuevas en este listado son los UDG (User Definable Graphics) y algunas detecciones de colisión básicas. Por lo tanto lo repasaramos brevemente. También es nuevo el uso de valores vectoriales direccionales almacenados en vx y vy, que aumentan o disminuyen constantemente los valores de 'x' y 'y' para el movimiento de la bola añadiéndose (vx o vy) a 'x' o 'y' en cada loop.

```
4010 LET bx=bx+vx: LET by=by+vy
```

Entonces ¿qué son UDGs?

UDG significa User Defined Graphics (gráficos definidos por el usuario) y ayudan a agregar sprites gráficos a un juego. Las líneas 7010 a 7050 buscan valores para colocarlos en la memoria y así crear UDG. Mientras, las líneas 7300 mantienen los datos que componen los valores para entrar en la memoria UDG.

```
7010 FOR n = 0 TO 31
7020 READ graph
7030 POKE USR "a"+n,graph
7050 NEXT n
```

El comando READ busca las sentencias DATA en su código. Este lee en orden cada valor dentro de las sentencias DATA y, si se queda sin datos, entonces se produce un error. Así que asegúrate de introducir todos los valores de datos. Puedes decirle a READ dónde comenzar a usar RESTORE <data_line_number>. Los UDG son caracteres gráficos dentro del conjunto de caracteres, que por defecto se parecen a los mismos que las letras de la A a la Z. Después de algunos POKE bien pensados, estas letras se pueden cambiar a gráficos. Cada carácter UDG tiene 8 bytes y cada byte contiene 8 bits.

Una forma fácil de crear estos gráficos es utilizando la función BIN, que no es más que una abreviatura para binario. La función BIN cubrirá una cadena de 1s y 0s en un número decimal.

Los binarios en el Spectrum oscilan desde 0 a 255. Cada dígito 0 o 1 representa un número que duplica el valor del dígito anterior.

Dígito 1	Dígito 2	Dígito 3	Dígito 4	Dígito 5	Dígito 6	Dígito 7	Dígito 8
1 = 1	1 = 2	1 = 4	1 = 8	1 = 16	1 = 32	1 = 64	1 = 128

Los 8 dígitos (de derecha a izquierda) suman 255. A continuación se muestra un ejemplo de datos binarios para crear una forma básica de árbol y los equivalentes decimales de cada byte de la UDG. Un UDG contiene 8 bytes de datos. Ejemplo: BIN 00000011 = 3

He aquí un ejemplo de cómo luce un Binario => Decimal

```
                          87654321
0 0 0 1 1 1 0 0          00011100          28
0 0 1 0 1 0 1 0          00101010          42
0 1 0 0 1 0 0 1          01001001          73
0 0 0 1 1 1 0 0          00011100          28
0 0 1 0 1 0 1 0          00101010          42
0 1 0 0 1 0 0 1          01001001          73
0 0 0 1 1 1 0 0          00011100          28
0 0 1 1 1 1 1 0          00111110          62
```

Consejo: Usar código para crear UDG es relativamente fácil. USR "a" es el primer carácter UDG.

```
7010 FOR n = 0 TO 7
7020 READ graph
7030 POKE USR "a"+n,graph
7050 NEXT n
7060 RETURN
7200 DATA BIN 00111100, BIN 01100110, BIN 01011110, BIN
01011110, BIN 01111110, BIN 00111100, BIN 00000000, BIN
00000000
```

Sugerencias para ampliar el juego (opcional)

1]   *Añadir más formaciones de nivel*

2]   *Añadir poderes*

SNAKE BITE

Debes ayudar a la serpiente a sobrevivir, mientras crece al comer las manzanas que caen de los árboles. Trata de comer el mayor número posible de estas frutas sin chocar contra los lados de la pantalla o tu propia cola ¡Buena suerte! Yo y mis compañeros de clase pasábamos horas jugando este juego de DOS en nuestras IBM durante las clases de informática. Luego apareció en los teléfonos Nokia y fue uno de los primeros juegos en teléfonos móviles.

Jugadores: 1

Reglas: El jugador trata de comer tantas manzanas como sea posible y superar la puntuación más alta. Chocar contra los bordes o contra tu propia cola terminará el juego.

Controles: q = arriba, a = abajo, o = izquierda, p = derecha.

```
 10 REM ******ZX Spectrum Code Club *******
 15 REM * SNAKE BITE by Gary Plowman 2015 *
 20 REM *********************************
 25 LET hsc=0: GO SUB 6000:
 30 INK 1: PAPER 7: BORDER 4: CLS
 45 REM ****** Initialising variables
 50 PRINT AT 2,10; INK 7; BRIGHT 1; PAPER 2;"SNAKE BITE":
PRINT AT 4,5;"Control your snake *"
 35 LET lives=3
 60 PRINT AT 7,5;"Avoid your tail! *****"
 65 PRINT AT 8,5;"Eat the apples"; PAPER 6;"o"
 70 PRINT AT 11,2;"Controls: ";AT 12,2;"Q/A=Up/Down,
O/P=Left/Right"
 80 PRINT AT 18,5; FLASH 1;"PRESS A KEY TO START": PAUSE 0
```

```
 100 GO SUB 300: REM initialise
 130 GO SUB 1000: REM main loop for game
 200 GO TO 30:
 300 REM *** SETUP
 310 LET x=10: LET y=10: LET vx=0: LET vy=0: LET score=0: LET
lvl=1: LET ax=1: LET ay=1: LET ax2=0: LET ay2=0: LET loot=0:
LET snk = 5: LET dx=x-5: LET dy=y: LET longer=0: LET snkpos=1:
LET ny=0: LET nx=0: LET ly=0: LET lx=0
 330 RETURN
1000 CLS
1010 FOR n = 0 TO 19:
1030 PRINT AT n,0;CHR$ (136);AT n,31;CHR$ (136)
1040 NEXT n
1045 FOR n=1 TO 30
1050 PRINT AT 0,n;CHR$ (136);AT 19,n;CHR$ (136)
1060 NEXT n
1087 PRINT AT INT (RND*15)+3,INT (RND*25)+3; PAPER 6;"o"
1095 PRINT AT 20,1;"Score: ";score
1096 FOR n=1 TO 5
1097 PRINT AT y,x-n;"*"
1098 NEXT n
1099 PRINT AT y,x;"*"
1100 LET i$=INKEY$(): LET i=IN 31
1110 IF (i$="q" OR i=8) AND y>2 THEN LET vy=-1: LET vx=0
1120 IF (i$="a" OR i=4) AND y<19 THEN LET vy=1: LET vx=0
1130 IF (i$="o" OR i=1) AND x>2 THEN LET vx=-1: LET vy=0
1140 IF (i$="p" OR i=2) AND y<30 THEN LET vx=1: LET vy=0
1145 LET x=x+vx: LET y  =y+vy
1150 IF x=0 THEN GO SUB 2000
1160 IF x=31 THEN GO SUB 2000
1170 IF y=19 THEN GO SUB 2000
1180 IF y=0 THEN GO SUB 2000
1185 LET a$=SCREEN$ (y,x)
1200 IF a$="o" THEN GO SUB 3000
1210 IF vx<>0 OR vy<>0 THEN GO SUB 2500
1230 PRINT AT y,x;"*"
```

```
1300 GO TO 1100
1900 STOP
2000 PRINT AT 10,10;"DEAD!";AT 15,10; FLASH 1;"RESTARTING":
BEEP 2,1: PAUSE 1000
2010 IF score>hsc THEN LET hsc=score
2100 GO TO 30
2500 REM *** DRAW SNAKE
2510 IF a$="*" AND (vx<>0 OR vy<>0) THEN GO SUB 2000
2520 PRINT AT dy,dx;" ":
2525 IF longer>0 THEN LET longer=longer-1: RETURN
2526 LET mx=0: LET nx=0: LET ny=0
2530 IF SCREEN$ (dy-1,dx)="*" THEN LET ny=-1: LET mx=mx+1
2540 IF SCREEN$ (dy+1,dx)="*" THEN LET ny=1: LET mx=mx+1
2550 IF SCREEN$ (dy,dx-1)="*" THEN LET nx=-1: LET mx=mx+1
2560 IF SCREEN$ (dy,dx+1)="*" THEN LET nx=1: LET mx=mx+1
2570 IF mx>1 THEN GO SUB 4000
2575 LET dy = dy + ny: LET dx=dx+nx
2580 RETURN
3000 REM *** EAT APPLE
3010 LET score = score +(INT (RND*4)+1)
3020 PRINT AT 20,1; PAPER 1; INK 7;"Score: ";score;AT
20,16;"Hi-Score: ";hsc: BEEP .05,20
3030 LET ax=INT (RND*25)+3: LET ay=INT (RND*15)+3
3040 IF SCREEN$ (ay,ax)="*" THEN GO TO 3030
3050 PRINT AT ay,ax; PAPER 6;"o": BEEP .1,1: LET longer=2
3060 RETURN
4000 REM *** Follow correct route
4010 LET r1=0: LET r2=0
4020 IF SCREEN$ (dy+ny,dx)="*" THEN LET r1=r1+1
4030 IF SCREEN$ (dy+(ny*2),dx)="*" THEN LET r1=r1+1
4040 IF SCREEN$ (dy+(ny*3),dx)="*" THEN LET r1=r1+1
4050 IF SCREEN$ (dy,dx+nx)="*" THEN LET r2=r2+1
4060 IF SCREEN$ (dy,dx+(nx*2))="*" THEN LET r2=r2+1
4070 IF SCREEN$ (dy,dx+(nx*3))="*" THEN LET r2=r2+1
4075 IF r1>r2 THEN LET nx=0: LET ly=ny: LET lx=0: RETURN
4080 IF r1<r2 THEN LET ny=0: LET lx=nx: LET ly=0: RETURN
```

```
4090 IF r1=r2 THEN LET nx=lx: LET ny=ly
4095 PRINT AT 19,10;"R1=";r1;" R2=";r2
4100 RETURN
7000 FOR n = 0 TO 7
7010 READ dat
7020 POKE USR "a"+n,dat
7030 NEXT n
7040 RETURN
7050 DATA 16,60,66,218,75,66,60,8
```

¿Qué hay de nuevo?

Aquí lo nuevo es un segundo método para los controles. IN 31 se utiliza para leer el puerto Joystick de la máquina (o emulador). Así que ahora tendrás la posibilidad de usar mandos joystick en tus propios juegos. Sí, es muy fácil agregar controles de joystick a un juego de Sinclair BASIC. Las líneas 1100 a 1140 contienen el código para detectar controles de teclado y joystick para tu juego. ¡Son sólo 5 líneas de código!

```
1100 LET i$=INKEY$(): LET i=IN 31
1110 IF (i$="q" OR i=8) AND y>2 THEN LET vy=-1: LET vx=0
1120 IF (i$="a" OR i=4) AND y<19 THEN LET vy=1: LET vx=0
1130 IF (i$="o" OR i=1) AND x>2 THEN LET vx=-1: LET vy=0
1140 IF (i$="p" OR i=2) AND y<30 THEN LET vx=1: LET vy=0
```

Para utilizar una o más opciones de puertos de joystick en Sinclair, sólo necesitas las teclas de configuración 1,2,3,4 y 5 o 6,7,8,9 y 0. Estas teclas serán equivalentes a izquierda, derecha, abajo, arriba y disparar.

Velocidad

Con el fin de mantener el juego en funcionamiento a la misma velocidad de principio a fin (sin ningún código en la máquina) hemos utilizado una rutina de alimentación de personalizada para nuestra serpiente y, para permitir que la serpiente crezca, retrasamos la rutina de alimentación cada vez que la serpiente come.

Detección de colisiones

Los comandos como SCREEN$ (dy+ny,dx)= "*" pueden ser útiles para probar la colisión o dejar que el programa sepa a dónde se pueden mover los objetos o si parte de la pantalla está vacía o no. Ten esto en cuenta cuando estés creando tus propios juegos.

Altas puntuaciones

Mi registro personal en esta versión del juego es 72. ¡Trata de superarlo!

SI x ENTONCES y

Todos los juegos necesitan tomar decisiones. Estas decisiones en BASIC se realizan utilizando sentencias IF THEN. SI x=1 ENTONCES hacer algo: ahora hacer otra cosa: y así sucesivamente. Las sentencias IF en Sinclair BASIC son bastante simples y ejecutan sólo una sola línea de comandos. No tienen las condiciones alternativas ELSE o ELSEIF. Sin embargo, pueden ramificarse y realizar varios comandos con GOTO o GO SUB. A lo largo de este libro también veremos sentencias IF con condiciones múltiples para cumplir con las expresiones Booleanas AND/OR.

Ejemplo de expresión booleana simple

Entre IF y THEN podrás tener una serie de expresiones diferentes que puedes probar como TRUE o FALSE y puedes combinar y ordenar esas expresiones utilizando paréntesis y operadores booleanos de AND y OR.

La expresión AND devuelve TRUE si ambos lados son TRUE:
1 Y 1 = TRUE   1 Y 0 = FALSE

La expresión OR devuelve TRUE si al menos un lado es TRUE:

1 O 0 = TRUE   0 O 0 = FALSE

Con estos agregados, tu sentencia se convertirá en algo como esto:

IF (a=x OR b=x) AND c=x THEN y

En la línea anterior, las expresiones entre paréntesis son comprobadas primero, luego su resultado es comprobado contra la última expresión usando el operador AND.

Otro operador booleano que puedes utilizar es NOT. Esto invierte el resultado de la expresión con la que se utiliza, por lo que NOT 1=1 equivaldría como FALSE en lugar de TRUE y la expresión NOT 1=0 equivaldría como TRUE.

Sonidos básicos de BEEP

El comando BEEP es agradable y sencillo. Tiene dos ajustes BEEP: duración y tono.

Aquí hay una escala de Piano simple para algunos de los valores de BEEP.

...	C	C#	D	D#	E	F	F#	G	G#	A	A#	B	C	...
←	0	1	2	3	4	5	6	7	8	9	10	11	12	→

La duración se mide en segundos o fracciones de segundo. Ejemplo: 5 segundos.

Así que para aquellos que son músicos, podéis tratar de añadir algo de música a vuestros juegos.

El modo 128k ofrece otra opción en forma de comando PLAY que utiliza el chip AY, que es más musical, pero para facilitar su uso y compatibilidad, utilizaremos simplemente BEEP.

Sugerencias para ampliar el juego (opcional)

1]   Agregar UDG y utilizar atributos de color para detección
de colisiones

2]   Añadir más obstáculos

3]   Añadir temporizador para ejercer más presión sobre el jugador y deba
actuar rápidamente

FLAPPY BIRD

El mundo se volvió loco con Flappy en 2014. Flappy Bird estaba en todas partes y, con la noticia de que el desarrollador creó el juego en muy poco tiempo, miles de nuevos programadores entraron en escena. Se generó nuevamente un interés en la 'programación de dormitorio' en muchos países del mundo. Creé una versión en BASIC ese mismo año, sólo por diversión. No es tan rápido como el original pero ¿a quién le importa? Aún así es Flappy Bird, especialmente si aumentas la velocidad del emulador. ¡Disfrútalo!

Jugadores: 1

Reglas: El jugador intenta atravesar las tuberías que se aproximan sin chocar contra ellas. En cada turno el jugador trata de superar su puntuación más alta.

Controles: Presiona cualquier tecla para permanecer en el aire. ¡Nada más!

```
  1 REM Speccy Conversion by G Plowman ( Gazzapper Games)
  2 PRINT AT 10,10;"LOADING GRAPHICS"
  3 GO SUB 3000
  5 BRIGHT 1
  6 PAPER 7
  7 INK 1: CLS
  8 LET hscore=0
 10 PRINT AT 1,0: INK 2: PRINT "===  =   ==== ====  ====  =
="
 20 INK 3: PRINT "=    =   = ==  == ==  = = ="
 21 INK 4: PRINT "===  =   ==== ====  ====  ===="
 22 INK 5: PRINT "=    =   = ==    =      ="
 24 INK 1: PRINT "=    =   = ==    =      ="
 26 INK 3: PRINT "=    =   = ==    =      ="
```

```
 28 INK 2: PRINT "=     === = = =      =         ="
 30 PRINT ""
 32 INK 4: PRINT "====  == ==== ==="
 34 INK 2: PRINT "=  =  == =  = =  ="
 36 INK 1: PRINT "====  == ==== =   ="
 38 INK 4: PRINT "=  =  == = =  =   ="
 40 INK 3: PRINT "=  =  == =  = =   ="
 42 INK 5: PRINT "====  == =  = ==="
 43 PRINT "": INK 0
 48 PRINT "SINCLAIR SPECTRUM CONVERSION"
 49 PRINT "By Gary Plowman- Orig .Gears"
 50 PRINT
 51 PRINT " PRESS A KEY TO START"
 53 PRINT " (CONTROLS : ANY KEY TO FLY"
 55 LET b$=""   : LET c$=""
 56 FOR n=1 TO 30: LET b$=b$+CHR$ (132): LET c$=c$+CHR$ (136)
: NEXT n
 58 INK 3: PRINT AT 19,0;b$
 60 FOR n=1 TO 30
 62 PRINT AT 1,n;" ";CHR$ (144)
 64 PAUSE 5
 66 PRINT AT 1,n;" ";CHR$ (145)
 68 BEEP .02,1
 70 PAUSE 5
 75 IF INKEY$<>"" THEN GO TO 200
 80 NEXT n
 85 PRINT AT 1,n;"   ":
 86 GO TO 60
200 LET score=INT (0): LET r=1
202 DIM x(10): DIM h(10)
203 LET pipes=1
204 LET fly=12: LET anim=0
205 BRIGHT 1: PAPER 7: INK 2
206 CLS
210 PRINT AT 10,10;"G E T   R E A D Y!"
```

```
220 PRINT ""
222 INK 1: PRINT AT 12,10;"  ";CHR$ (144)
226 PRINT
227 INK 2: PRINT "      Tap To Fly"
230 IF INKEY$="" THEN GO TO 230
300 REM ****** START **********
302 FOR o=1 TO 10
303 LET h(o)=INT (RND*8)+1
305 NEXT o
306 FOR l=1 TO 10
308 LET x(l)=25+(l*5)
309 NEXT l
310 GO SUB 1000
600 GO TO 310
999 REM **********************
1000 REM **** DRAW PIPES
1002 CLS
1010 INK 1: PRINT AT fly,10;"  ";CHR$ (144): LET fly=fly+1
1011 INK 3: PLOT 0,20: DRAW 240,0
1012 IF anim=1 THEN INK 1: PRINT AT fly-1,10;"  ";CHR$ (145)
1013 LET anim=0
1016 LET r=r+1
1017 INK 3: PRINT AT 0,2;"SCORE: ";score: PRINT AT 0,20;"HI-
SCORE:";hscore
1018 IF INKEY$<>"" THEN LET fly=fly-2: BEEP .01,2
1030 FOR p=1 TO 10
1033 IF INKEY$<>"" THEN LET anim=1
1035 INK 4
1039 LET bh=h(p)*8: IF x(p)<30 AND x(p)>1 AND h(p)>0 THEN PLOT
x(p)*8,3*8: DRAW 0,bh: DRAW 8,0: DRAW 0,-(bh)
1040 LET nh=INT ((13-(h(p)))*8): IF x(p)<30 AND x(p)>1 AND
h(p)>0 THEN PLOT x(p)*8,150: DRAW 0,-nh: DRAW 8,0: DRAW 0,nh
1041 IF x(p)<1 THEN LET h(p)=INT (RND*8)+1
1042 IF x(p)<1 THEN LET x(p)=40
1050 REM INK 3: IF p=4 THEN PRINT AT 19,0;c$
1052 LET x(p)=x(p)-1
```

```
1059 IF x(p)=9 AND h(p)>0 THEN BEEP .02,3: LET score=score+1
1070 IF x(p)=12 AND fly>19-h(p) THEN GO SUB 1200
1075 IF x(p)=12 AND fly<19-(h(p)+3) THEN GO SUB 1200
1076 IF fly=20 THEN GO SUB 1200
1080 NEXT p
1100 RETURN
1200 REM **** DEAD ****
1210 PRINT AT 10,4;"OUCH!!"
1220 BEEP .3,7: BEEP .3,2: BEEP .5,-3
1240 PRINT AT 12,4;"HIT ENTER TO RESTART!"
1300 IF INKEY$=CHR$ (13) THEN GO TO 200
1310 GO TO 1300
3000 LET daa=0
3002 FOR n=0 TO 167
3005 READ DAA
3010 DATA
12,18,37,193,254,66,60,0,12,18,37,193,254,126,0,0,0,60,66,64,6
4,66,60,0,0,120,68,66,66,68,120,0,0,126,64,124,64,64,126,0,0,1
26,64,124,64,64,64,0,0,60,66,64,78,66,60,0,0,66,66,126,66,66,6
6,0,0,62,8,8,8,8,62,0,0,2,2,2,66,66,60,0,0,68,72,112,72,68,66,
0,0,64,64,64,64,64,126,0,0,66,102,90,66,66,66,0,0,66,98,82,74,
70,66,0,0,60,66,66,66,66,60,0,0,124,66,66,124,64,64,0,0,60,66,
66,82,74,60,0,0,124,66,66,124,68,66,0,0,60,64,60,2,66,60,0,0,2
54,16,16,16,16,16,0,0,66,66,66,66,66,60,0,0
3030 POKE USR "a"+n,daa
3040 NEXT n
3050 RETURN
```

¿Qué hay de nuevo?

Ahora que ya has escrito una versión de Flappy Bird en el Spectrum, podrás ver cómo un juego tan divertido se puede hacer con un código tan sencillo. Bueno, tal vez algunas partes del código son un poco confusas, pero probablemente sea debido al uso de las matemáticas. Es bastante fácil una vez explicado. La detección de colisión de pantalla para las tuberías se multiplicaron por 8 para permitir que las tuberías se dibujen en la cuadrícula de pantalla de píxeles de 256 (eje x) por 192 píxeles (eje y). Pero la detección de colisión real se basó en la cuadrícula de impresión de caracteres de 32 (eje x) por 22 posiciones de carácter (eje Y). Para que sea más fácil de entender, comparando las ubicaciones de impresión de caracteres con las ubicaciones de píxeles, necesitamos multiplicar o dividir por o entre un factor de 8. Por cada 8 píxeles hay 1 posición de carácter. Consulta el siguiente diagrama para saber cómo funciona la pantalla para píxeles y caracteres.

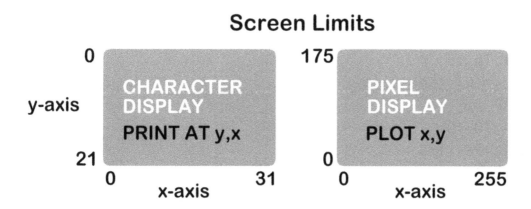

Hola Colour Clash

Una limitación conocida del Sinclair Spectrum es que sólo pueden existir dos colores dentro de cada posición de carácter en la pantalla (8 x 8 píxeles). Esto agrega un poco de retro-encanto a los juegos cuando se mezclan. Notarás esta característica en este juego mientras tu Flappy Bird choca contra las tubos. Ahí lo puedes ver: ¡eso es colour clash!

Animación básica

La animación con UDG (también conocida como Sprites) se ejecuta muy sencillamente aquí.

```
1033 IF INKEY$<>"" THEN LET anim=1
```

La línea anterior establece el valor de anim a 1 para que sepamos dibujar el sprite UDG del aleteo del pájaro, lo que hacen que nuestro pájaro mueva sus alas.

```
1012 IF anim=1 THEN INK 1: PRINT AT fly-1,10;"  ";CHR$ (145)
```

Este es un método muy sencillo y fácil. Hacer más de un marco de animación implica el seguimiento de movimiento con un valor de temporizador. Pero ese nivel de detalle es para explicar en otro momento. La primera parte del comando PRINT borra la posición antigua de nuestro pájaro antes de imprimir la nueva posición.

```
302 FOR o=1 TO 10
303 LET h(o)=INT (RND*8)+1
305 NEXT o
306 FOR l=1 TO 10
308 LET x(l)=25+(l*5)
309 NEXT l
```

El código anterior crea las posiciones de tubería y sus alturas, pero no las mostrará hasta que se hayan desplazado lo suficiente como para mostrarse en nuestra pantalla.

Sugerencias para ampliar el juego (opcional)

1]   *Añadir enemigos*

2]   *¡Quita las tuberías superiores y trabaja en un clon Scramble!*

THE NUMBERS GAME

Me encanta "8 Out of 10 Cats Does Countdown", así como resolver problemas matemáticos. Este juego es básicamente eso. No es muy avanzado, por lo tanto puedes intentar resolver tus propios problemas. Tal vez puedas inspirarte para crear la versión con palabras en un futuro.

Jugadores: 1

Reglas: El jugador intenta calcular el resultado usando comandos matemáticos y los números proporcionados y.

Controles: Escribir los respectivos valores y comandos: 'add', 'mult' y 'sub'.

```
  10 REM **********ZX CODE CLUB***************
  15 REM * The Numbers Game (Countdown)        *
  20 REM ***********G.Plowman******************
  30 INK 0: PAPER 5: BORDER 4: CLS
  45 REM ****** Initialising variables
  50 PRINT AT 2,7; INK 7; BRIGHT 1; PAPER 7; INK 3;"The
Numbers Game": PRINT AT 4,5;""
  60 PRINT AT 4,5;"Mathletes Get Ready!"
  80 PRINT AT 18,5; FLASH 1;"PRESS A KEY TO START": PAUSE 0:
CLS
 100 REM GO SUB 5000: REM Graphics
 110 GO SUB 300: REM initialise:
 130 GO SUB 1000: REM draw screen
 140 GO SUB 2000: main loop
 300 REM **** init
 310 LET p1=0: LET p2=0: LET p3=0: LET p4=0: LET p5=0: LET
p$="": LET q$="": LET r$="":
```

```
 320 LET s$="": LET t$="":
 330 RETURN
1000 REM ****** Screen
1005 PRINT AT 3,10; PAPER 7; BRIGHT 1; INK 3;"THE NUMBERS
GAME"
1010 FOR n=5 TO 10
1020 PRINT AT n,10; PAPER 7;"                    "
1030 NEXT n
1040 PRINT AT 5,3; INK 6;CHR$ (137);CHR$ (143);CHR$ (143);CHR$
(143);CHR$ (134)
1060 PRINT AT 6,2; INK 6;CHR$ (133); PAPER 7; CHR$ (138);CHR$
(137);" ";CHR$ (137); INK 6;CHR$ (133); PAPER 5;CHR$ (138)
1070 PRINT AT 7,2; INK 6;CHR$ (133); PAPER 7;CHR$ (138); INK
1;CHR$ (132);" ";CHR$ (132); INK 6;CHR$ (133); PAPER 5;CHR$
(138)
1080 PRINT AT 8,2; INK 6;CHR$ (133); PAPER 7;CHR$ (138);"    ";
PAPER 5;CHR$ (143)
1090 PRINT AT 9,2; INK 6;CHR$ (133); PAPER 7;CHR$ (138); INK
2;CHR$ (132);CHR$ (140);" "; INK 6; PAPER 5;CHR$ (143)
1100 PRINT AT 10,3; INK 6;CHR$ (133); PAPER 7;CHR$ (138);" ";
INK 6;CHR$ (133)
1110 PRINT AT 11,4; PAPER 7;"   "
1200 FOR n = 12 TO 18
1205 RANDOMIZE
1210 LET c=INT (RND*4)+3
1215 PRINT AT n+1,3; INK INT (RND*4);CHR$ (143);CHR$
(143);CHR$ (143);AT n,4;CHR$ (143);CHR$ (143);;AT n+1,5;CHR$
(143);CHR$ (143)
1230 NEXT n
1250 FOR n=13 TO 19 STEP 2
1260 PRINT AT n,14; PAPER 7;"  "; PAPER 5;" "; PAPER 7;"  ";
PAPER 5;" "; PAPER 7;"   "; PAPER 5;" "; PAPER 7;"   "
1270 NEXT n
2000 PRINT AT 1,10;"PRESS S TO START"
2010 LET i$=INKEY$()
2020 IF i$="s" THEN GO TO 2100
```

```
2030 GO TO 2010
2100 RANDOMIZE
2105 LET ans=0: LET ans1=0
2110 LET n1=INT (RND*90)+10
2120 LET n2=INT (RND*10)+2
2130 LET n3=INT (RND*10)+2
2140 LET n4=INT (RND*10)+2
2150 LET n5=INT (RND*10)+2
2170 LET o1=INT (RND*4)+1
2180 LET o2=INT (RND*4)+1
2190 LET o3=INT (RND*4)+1
2195 LET o4=INT (RND*4)+1:
2200 PRINT PAPER 1; INK 7;AT 8,12;n1; PAPER 7;" "; PAPER 1;n2;
PAPER 7;" "; PAPER 1;n3; PAPER 7;" "; PAPER 1;n4; PAPER 7;" ";
PAPER 1;n5; PAPER 7;" ":
2210 IF o1=1 THEN LET ans=n1-n2
2220 IF o1=2 THEN LET ans=n1*n2
2230 IF o1>2 THEN LET ans=n1+n2
2240 IF o2=1 AND n3>n4 THEN LET ans1=n3-n4
2245 IF o2=1 AND n3<n4 THEN LET ans1=n4-n3
2250 IF o2=2 THEN LET ans1=n3*n4
2260 IF o2>2 THEN LET ans1=n3-n4:
2270 IF o3=1 THEN LET ans=ans+ans1-n5
2280 IF o3=2 THEN LET ans=ans*n5+ans1
2290 IF o3>2 THEN LET ans=ans+ans1+n5
2295 IF ans<100 THEN GO TO 2100:
2300 PRINT AT 6,12;ans
2310 INPUT "Enter a number from the cards above:",p1
2315 IF p1<>n1 AND p1<>n2 AND p1<>n3 AND p1<>n4 AND p1<>n5
THEN BEEP .5,0: PRINT AT 11,10;"WRONG NUMBER": GO TO 2310
2320 INPUT "Enter command add,sub or mult:", LINE p$
2330 INPUT "Enter next number from the cards above:",p2
2335 IF p2<>n1 AND p2<>n2 AND p2<>n3 AND p2<>n4 AND p2<>n5
THEN BEEP .5,0: PRINT AT 11,10;"WRONG NUMBER": GO TO 2330
2340 INPUT "Enter command add, sub, mult or calc:", LINE q$
2345 IF q$="calc" THEN GO SUB 3000
```

```
2350 INPUT "Enter next number from the cards above:",p3
2355 IF p3<>n1 AND p3<>n2 AND p3<>n3 AND p3<>n4 AND p3<>n5
THEN BEEP .5,0: PRINT AT 11,10;"WRONG NUMBER": GO TO 2350
2360 INPUT "Enter command add, sub, mult or calc:", LINE r$
2370 IF r$="calc" THEN GO SUB 3000
2380 INPUT "Enter next number from the cards above:",p4
2385 IF p4<>n1 AND p4<>n2 AND p4<>n3 AND p4<>n4 AND p4<>n5
THEN BEEP .5,0: PRINT AT 11,10;"WRONG NUMBER": GO TO 2380
2390 INPUT "Enter command add, sub, mult or calc:", LINE s$
2400 IF s$="calc" THEN GO SUB 3000
2410 INPUT "Enter next number from the cards above:",p5
2420 IF p5<>n1 AND p5<>n2 AND p5<>n3 AND p5<>n4 AND p5<>n5
THEN BEEP .5,0: PRINT AT 11,10;"WRONG NUMBER": GO TO 2380:
2440 IF p$="calc" THEN GO SUB 3000:
2490 GO SUB 3000
3000 REM ***** CHECK ANSWER
3010 LET answer=0
3020 IF p$="add" THEN LET answer = p1+p2
3030 IF p$="sub" THEN LET answer = p1-p2
3040 IF p$="mult" THEN LET answer= p1*p2
3050 IF q$="add" THEN LET answer = answer+ p3
3060 IF q$="sub" THEN LET answer = answer-p3
3070 IF q$="mult" THEN LET answer= answer*p3
3080 IF r$="add" THEN LET answer = answer+p4
3090 IF r$="sub" THEN LET answer = answer-p4
3100 IF r$="mult" THEN LET answer= answer*p4
3110 IF s$="add" THEN LET answer = answer+p5
3120 IF s$="sub" THEN LET answer = answer-p5
3130 IF s$="mult" THEN LET answer= answer*p5
3200 IF answer = ans THEN BEEP 1,6: PRINT AT 11,10; INK
1;"Yay! ";answer;" is correct!"
3210 IF answer<>ans THEN BEEP 1,-7: PRINT AT 11,10; INK 2;"You
Got ";answer;"     "
3250 PRINT AT 12,10;"Press to Play Again": PAUSE 0
3260 GO TO 1000
```

Progreso

Y bueno ¿cómo te va tratando BASIC? A estas alturas del libro ya deberías entender determinados comandos y para qué se utilizan. También habrás notado muchos códigos de Caracteres en la última lista. Estos pueden ser consultados al final del libro en el Apéndice A.

Input

Utilizamos una cantidad considerable de comandos INPUT. Este es un comando muy útil para pedir al usuario que realice acciones o tome decisiones. Es muy útil para juegos de aventuras con texto o historias interactivas donde las decisiones de los usuarios pueden cambiar la ruta de la historia.

PEEKs y POKEs

Para nuestros gráficos UDG utilizamos un comando llamado POKE. Este comando coloca un valor decimal en una posición de memoria. Luego podemos recopilar este valor de nuevo utilizando un comando PEEK.

Ejemplo: Prueba POKE 33000,45 luego enter, ahora intente PEEK 33000 para recuperar el valor.

Funciones matemáticas

Sinclair BASIC tiene muchas funciones matemáticas. No es perfecto, ni tiene todas las funciones, pero tiene la mayoría de trigonometría simple o Algebra que un principiante necesitaría. Ejemplos: PI (3.141592 ... etc), EXP (Exponencial), LN (Logaritmos), SIN (Seno), COS (Coseno), TAN (Tangente).

Sugerencias para ampliar el juego (opcional)

1]   Añadir soluciones matemáticas más complejas

2]   Añadir la versión de letras/palabras al juego

BATTLESHIP WAR

Otro juego clásico de bolígrafo y papel. Battleship War es la versión computarizada de este juego, pero con algunas pequeñas enmiendas. Elije tu cuadrícula para colocar tus barcos. Asegúrate que tu oponente no vea la pantalla. Luego, cuando hayas terminado será el turno de tu contrincante para poner sus barcos en su cuadrícula. El ganador será jugador que destruya todos los barcos de su oponente. ¡Vamos allá!

Jugadores: 2

Reglas: Coloca los barcos en la cuadrícula presionando las teclas para las coordenadas. El ganador será el jugador que destruya todos los barcos de su oponente.

Controles: Teclas A a J para colocación horizontal y 1 a 9 para colocación vertical en la cuadrícula o disparar. R para rotar la posición del barco antes de pulsar ENTER para colocar.

Consejo: Un trozo grande de cartón sirve para ocultar las pantallas durante el juego multijugador (hotseat).

```
10 REM ****** ZX Code Club **************
15 REM * BATTLESHIP WAR by Gary Plowman  *
20 REM ********************************
30 INK 7: PAPER 0: BORDER 4: CLS
40 PRINT AT 5,10; INK 2;"BATTLESHIP WAR"
50 PRINT AT 10,5;"2 Player Game (hotseat)"
60 PRINT AT 12,5; BRIGHT 1; INVERSE 1;"1. Start Game"
70 PRINT AT 15,2;"Use a card to hide some"
80 PRINT AT 16,2;"of the screen or look away"
```

```
  90 PRINT AT 17,2;"when other player is placing";AT
18,2;"their units":
 100 IF INKEY$="1" THEN LET gm=1: GO TO 130
 120 GO TO 100
 130 BEEP .2,7: BEEP .6,2: BEEP .3,-3: BEEP .7,9
 135 INPUT "ENTER # SHIPS EACH (2 to 5):";noships
 140 BORDER 5: CLS
 150 PRINT AT 1,10; INK 2;"BATTLESHIP WAR":
 160 GO SUB 190
 170 GO TO 270
 180 REM *********************** Redo Board *
 190 FOR n=6 TO 14
 200 PRINT AT n,5; PAPER 5; INK 1;"-----------"
 210 PRINT AT n,17; PAPER 5; INK 1;"-----------"
 220 PRINT AT n,3; PAPER 3;n-5;AT n,28;n-5
 230 NEXT n
 240 LET a$="ABCDEFGHIJ"
 250 PRINT AT 5,5;a$;AT 5,17;a$
 260 RETURN
 270 IF gm=2 THEN PRINT AT 18,3;"PLAYER 1 GET READY";AT
19,3;"PLAYER 2 LOOK AWAY"
 280 PRINT AT 21,5; FLASH 1;"PRESS KEY TO CONTINUE"
 290 IF INKEY$="" THEN GO TO 290
 300 GO SUB 320
 310 GO SUB 380
 320 REM *************** Clearing part of screen
 325 PRINT AT 17,0;"                              "
 330 PRINT AT 18,0;"                              "
 340 PRINT AT 19,0;"                              "
 350 PRINT AT 20,0;"                              "
 360 PRINT AT 21,0;"                              "
 370 RETURN
 380 REM *************** PLACING PLAYER 1 UNITS
 390 DIM a(noships,2,2): DIM h(2): DIM f(2): DIM x(noships,2):
DIM y(5): LET shp1=1: LET shp2=1: LET r=0: LET m$="": LET
ply=1
```

```
 400 PRINT AT 17,3;"Press Coords for ship ";shp1;AT 18,3;"e.g.
A5"
 410 LET i$=INKEY$()
 420 IF i$>="a" AND i$<="k" THEN LET a(shp1,1,ply)=(CODE
(i$))-96: LET m$=i$+STR$ (a(shp1,2,ply)): BEEP .05,6
 430 IF i$>="1" AND i$<="9" THEN LET a(shp1,2,ply)=VAL (i$):
LET m$=i$+STR$ (a(shp1,2,ply)): BEEP .05,7
 435 IF a(shp1,1,ply)=0 OR a(shp1,2,ply)=0 THEN GO TO 400
 440 IF ply=1 THEN PRINT AT 4,2;CHR$
(a(shp1,1,ply)+96);a(shp1,2,ply); INK 6;"  Ship# ";shp1
 445 IF ply=2 THEN PRINT AT 4,2;"            ";AT 4,17;CHR$
(a(shp1,1,ply)+96);a(shp1,2,ply); INK 6;"  Ship# ";shp1
 450 IF r=1 AND a(shp1,2,ply)>7 THEN LET r=NOT r
 460 IF i$="r" THEN LET r=NOT r
 470 IF r=0 AND a(shp1,1,ply)>7 THEN LET r=NOT r
 480 IF i$=CHR$ (13) AND a(shp1,2,ply)>0 AND a(shp1,1,ply)>0
THEN BEEP .3,2: LET shp1=shp1+1: GO SUB 320: REM ***********
clean part of screen / next unit
 490 IF shp1=noships+1 AND ply=1 THEN BEEP 1,7: BEEP .2,4: LET
shp1=1: LET ply=2: GO SUB 190
 500 IF shp1=noships+1 AND ply=2 THEN LET ply=1: BEEP 1,7:
BEEP .2,4: GO TO 1000
 505 IF a(shp1,2,ply)>0 AND a(shp1,1,ply)>0 THEN PRINT AT
20,0; INK 6;"[R] Rotate Ship";AT 21,0; FLASH 1;"[Enter] Next
Ship"
 510 IF a(shp1,1,ply)=0 OR a(shp1,2,ply)=0 THEN GO TO 400
 520 IF i$<>"" THEN GO SUB 190: REM *************** redo board
again *
 530 IF r=0 THEN LET x(shp1,ply)=0
 540 IF r=1 THEN LET x(shp1,ply)=1
 550 FOR n=1 TO shp1
 560 IF x(n,ply)=0 AND ply=1 THEN PRINT AT
a(n,2,ply)+5,a(n,1,ply)+4;"***"
 570 IF x(n,ply)=1 AND ply=1 THEN PRINT AT
a(n,2,ply)+5,a(n,1,ply)+4;"*";AT
a(n,2,ply)+6,a(n,1,ply)+4;"*";AT a(n,2,ply)+7,a(n,1,ply)+4;"*"
```

```
 580 IF x(n,ply)=0 AND ply=2 THEN PRINT AT
a(n,2,ply)+5,a(n,1,ply)+16;"***"
 590 IF x(n,ply)=1 AND ply=2 THEN PRINT AT
a(n,2,ply)+5,a(n,1,ply)+16;"*";AT
a(n,2,ply)+6,a(n,1,ply)+16;"*";AT
a(n,2,ply)+7,a(n,1,ply)+16;"*"
 600 NEXT n
 700 GO TO 400
1000 REM ***** TAKE TURNS
1005 LET hits=1: LET ply=1: LET hits1=1: LET hits2=1
1010 PRINT AT 4,2;"                        "
1020 GO SUB 190
1030 GO SUB 320
1040 PRINT AT 17,0;"PLAYER ";ply;"....FIRE SHOT..e.g. A5"
1050 GO SUB 2000: REM Get shot
2000 REM ****** Get Shot coords
2005 LET ply=ply+1
2006 IF ply>2 THEN LET ply=1
2008 PRINT AT 18,0;"Current Hits on Target: ";f(ply)
2010 LET i$=INKEY$()
2020 IF i$>="a" AND i$<="k" THEN LET h(1)=(CODE (i$))-96: LET
m$=i$+STR$ (h(1)): BEEP .05,6
2030 IF i$>="1" AND i$<="9" THEN LET h(2)=VAL (i$): LET
m$=i$+STR$ (h(2)): BEEP .05,7
2040 IF h(1)>0 AND h(2)>0 THEN PRINT AT 20,0; INK
6;"FIRING...";h(1);"-";h(2): GO SUB 2300: GO TO 1030: REM ****
Check for hits
2050 IF f(ply)=noships*3 THEN GO SUB 2200:
2100 GO TO 2010
2200 REM ***** WINNER!
2210 PRINT AT 10,10;"PLAYER ";ply;" WINS!"
2220 FOR n = 1 TO 10
2230 BEEP .1,n+RND*2
2240 NEXT n
2250 BEEP 1,2: PAUSE 0
2260 GO TO 30
```

```
2260 RETURN
2300 REM **** Hit checks ************************
2305 LET miss=1
2316 IF ply=1 AND ATTR (h(2)+5,h(1)+4)<>41 THEN BEEP .1,-2: GO
TO 2380
2317 IF ply=2 AND ATTR (h(2)+5,h(1)+16)<>41 THEN BEEP .1,-2:
GO TO 2380
2320 FOR n=1 TO noships
2330 IF h(1)=a(n,1,ply) AND h(2)=a(n,2,ply) THEN LET miss=0:
LET f(ply)=f(ply)+1
2345 IF x(n,ply)=0 AND (h(1)-1=a(n,1,ply) OR h(1)-
2=a(n,1,ply)) AND h(2)=a(n,2,ply) THEN LET miss=0: LET
f(ply)=f(ply)+1
2346 IF x(n,ply)=1 AND (h(2)-1=a(n,2,ply) OR h(2)-
2=a(n,2,ply)) AND h(1)=a(n,1,ply) THEN LET miss=0: LET
f(ply)=f(ply)+1
2350 NEXT n
2360 IF ply=1 AND miss=0 THEN PRINT AT 21,0; FLASH 1;"PLAYER 2
SHIP HIT!";AT h(2)+5,h(1)+4; PAPER 2;"*"
2370 IF ply=2 AND miss=0 THEN PRINT AT 21,0; FLASH 1;"PLAYER 1
SHIP HIT!";AT h(2)+5,h(1)+16; PAPER 2;"*"
2380 IF miss=1 AND ply=2 AND ATTR (h(2)+5,h(1)+16)=41 THEN
PRINT AT 21,0;"YOU MISSED:!          ";AT h(2)+5,h(1)+16;
INK 6;"+": BEEP .3,7
2390 IF miss=1 AND ply=1 AND ATTR (h(2)+5,h(1)+4)=41 THEN
PRINT AT 21,0;"YOU MISSED!:          ";AT h(2)+5,h(1)+4;
INK 6;"+": BEEP .3,2
2400 LET h(1)=0: LET h(2)=0
2410 RETURN
```

¿Qué hay de nuevo?

Aquí se utilizan muchos más comandos Array para poder mantener el estado y la ubicación de los buques. No te preocupes si el código Array es confuso. Los principiantes usan muy poco los Arrays hasta que obtienen algo de confianza y a partir de allí comienzan a experimentar con ellos.

Para más eficiencia, no necesitamos volver a dibujar algunas partes de la pantalla. Por lo tanto, lo podremos evitar mediante el borrado selectivo del área de la pantalla después de que se haya producido una acción. Trucos simples como este ayudarán a acelerar tus programas.

```
320 REM ************** Clearing part of screen
325 PRINT AT 17,0;"                         "
330 PRINT AT 18,0;"                         "
340 PRINT AT 19,0;"                         "
350 PRINT AT 20,0;"                         "
360 PRINT AT 21,0;"                         "
```

```
DIM a(noships,2,2)
```

El Array anterior se utiliza como un contenedor de almacenamiento para barcos (x buques), ubicación (2 valores 'x' e 'y'), jugador (2 jugadores).

También se utilizan los comandos CODE y STR$ para obtener coordenadas de cuadrícula a partir de valores de teclas. A continuación, utilizamos m$ para mostrar la coordenada seleccionada.

```
2020 IF i$>="a" AND i$<="k" THEN LET h(1)=(CODE (i$))-96: LET
m$=i$+STR$ (h(1))
```

El puntero de array se utiliza para trazar la posición y la rotación del barco, el cual se guarda en la array x (#, #). No te preocupes si las arrays son un poco confusas. Con suficiente práctica las empezarás a utilizar en tu propio código sin ningún problema.

Sugerencias para ampliar el juego (opcional)

1]   *Añadir opciones de jugador CPU*

2]   *Añadir gráficos UDG para los barcos*

CODEBREAK

Es la Segunda Guerra Mundial y el enemigo está enviando órdenes secretas a sus tropas. Tu misión es hackear el código para descifrar los mensajes. ¿Recuerdas un pequeño juego electrónico en el que tenías que resolver el código de colores? También había un juego de mesa para 2 jugadores llamado MasterMind, en el que un segundo jugador fijaba el código y te decía si habías sido capaz de descifrar la secuencia de manera correcta.

Jugadores: 1 o más (cooperativo)

Reglas: Turnos limitados para adivinar el código de color. Elige entre Rojo, Azul, Verde, Cian, Magenta(violeta) y Amarillo. La CPU indicará 'Y' con el número de colores correctos y en secuencia, y 'C' para el número de colores correctos.

Controles: Ingresa una secuencia de colores por turno usando las turnos anteriores para descifrar el código.

```
10 REM ******ZX Spectrum Code Club *******
15 REM * CODEBREAK by G Plowman 2015      *
20 REM *********************************
30 INK 1: PAPER 7: BORDER 4: CLS
35 REM POKE 23617,128: REM **** PUT CURSOR IN CAPS MODE
45 REM ****** Initialising variables
50 PRINT AT 2,10; INK 7; BRIGHT 1; PAPER 2;"CODEBREAK":
PRINT AT 4,5;"Find the Colour Code!":
60 PRINT AT 7,5;"Get code in sequence"
70 PRINT AT 8,5;"Enter Colours 1 at a time.":
```

```
  80 PRINT AT 18,5; FLASH 1;"PRESS A KEY TO START": PAUSE 0
 100 GO SUB 300: REM initialise
 130 GO SUB 1000: REM main loop for game
 200 GO TO 30:
 300 REM ***** SETUP
 310 LET turn=1: DIM c(4): DIM t(4): DIM a$(1,1): LET col=0:
LET colseq=0: LET codeseq=1
 330 RETURN
1000 PAPER 4: CLS
1010 RANDOMIZE
1020 FOR n = 1 TO 4
1030 LET c(n)=INT (RND*5)+1
1040 NEXT n:
1050 GO SUB 2000: REM **** CREATE BOARD:
1100 REM **** START GAME LOOP
1005 PRINT AT 0,4;"C o d e   B r e a k "
1110 PRINT AT 2,2;"Turn:";turn;AT 20,0;"Seq:";codeseq
1120 PRINT AT 18,0;"Enter each letter for code"
1130 INPUT "Enter either r,g,b,c,m,y",a$(1,1):
1140 IF a$(1,1)="r" THEN LET t(codeseq)=2
1150 IF a$(1,1)="b" THEN LET t(codeseq)=1
1160 IF a$(1,1)="g" THEN LET t(codeseq)=4
1170 IF a$(1,1)="y" THEN LET t(codeseq)=6
1180 IF a$(1,1)="m" THEN LET t(codeseq)=3
1190 IF a$(1,1)="c" THEN LET t(codeseq)=5
1390 LET codeseq=codeseq+1
1400 IF codeseq=5 THEN LET codeseq=1: GO SUB 4000: REM ***
check CODE
1900 GO TO 1100:
2000 FOR n = 1 TO 15
2010 PRINT AT 2+n,10; PAPER 7; BRIGHT 1;"[     ]"; PAPER 5;"
"; PAPER 6;"   "
2020 NEXT n
2030 REM FOR n = 1 TO 4: PRINT AT 2,10+n; INK c(n);CHR$ (143)
2040 REM NEXT n: rem **** Un-REM if you want to see code
2050 RETURN
```

```
4000 REM checking code value
4010 LET col=0: LET colseq=0
4020 FOR n = 1 TO 4
4030 IF t(n)=c(n) THEN LET colseq=colseq+1: GO TO 4050
4040 IF t(n)<>c(n) AND (t(n)=c(1) OR t(n)=c(2) OR t(n)=c(3) OR
t(n)=c(4)) THEN LET col=col+1
4050 NEXT n
4060 LET turn=turn+1
4070 PRINT AT  18-turn,18; PAPER 7;"Y=";colseq;" C=";col
4080 FOR n = 1 TO 4: PRINT AT 18-turn,10+n; PAPER t(n);" ":
NEXT n
4090 IF turn=15 THEN PRINT AT 10,10;" YOU LOSE ": GO SUB 4300:
4100 IF colseq=4 THEN PRINT AT 10,5;"CONGRATS CODEBREAKER!";AT
12,5;"PRESS TO PLAY AGAIN": PAUSE 0: GO TO 30
4110 RETURN
4300 REM Lost
4310 PRINT PAPER 7;AT 12,10;"            ";AT 13,10;"
";AT 14,10;"            "
4320 FOR n = 1 TO 4
4340 PRINT AT 13,12+n; PAPER c(n);" "
4350 NEXT n
4360 PAUSE 0
4370 GO TO 30
```

Sencillo pero divertido

Es un juego sencillo y colorido para uno o más jugadores. Estos pueden debatir y acordar los colores para usar en la secuencia. Las líneas 2030 y 2040 permiten un pequeño "modo de trampa", para comprobar que el programa esté funcionando correctamente. Para usarlo, necesitas quitar el REM al inicio de cada línea.

¿Qué hay de nuevo?

RANDOMIZE se utiliza para generar un nuevo valor Random Seed. Cuando se coloca después de las respuestas de los usuarios, hace que el programa sea mucho más

aleatorio al utilizar las funciones RND. Hemos encontrado otro uso para nuestro amigo el Array. Sin embargo, esta vez es un uso más sencillo y directo.

```
1180 IF a$(1,1)="m" THEN LET t(codeseq)=3
```

El array t() se utiliza para guardar nuestra secuencia de código como un valor numérico para cada color. Luego podremos comprobarlos para que el usuario sepa cómo se relaciona con **colseq** al contar coincidencias de secuencias y de color exactas; y con **col** al contar los colores presentes correctos.

```
4000 REM checking code value
4010 LET col=0: LET colseq=0
4020 FOR n = 1 TO 4
4030 IF t(n)=c(n) THEN LET colseq=colseq+1: GO TO 4050
4040 IF t(n)<>c(n) AND (t(n)=c(1) OR t(n)=c(2) OR t(n)=c(3) OR
t(n)=c(4)) THEN LET col=col+1
4050 NEXT n
```

Una nota sobre Debugging

Es una buena práctica utilizar PRINT y otros comandos para recibir información clave al depurar los programas. Otro comando muy útil es STOP. Puedes utilizarlo con una instrucción IF para buscar y probar ciertas condiciones que desees evitar o corregir. STOP finalizará el programa en esa línea y devolverá al usuario al prompt BASIC.

Sugerencias para ampliar el juego (opcional)

1] Añadir más color y gráficos al juego en general

2] Añadir una opción de 2 jugadores donde un jugador pueda elegir el código

ASTRAL INVADERS

¡Prepárate para defender tu base! ¡Los alienígenas atacan! ¿Cuánto tiempo puedes sobrevivir a la embestida de estos alienígenas que han llegado para esclavizar a tu pueblo? El modo de juego de Space Invaders nunca envejece y casi todo el mundo ha disfrutado de alguna versión de este clásico juego de los 80s. El juego es divertido y adictivo, con gráficos UDG coloridos y agradables. Ahora, empecemos con la programación y vamos a matar alienígenas.

Jugadores: 1

Reglas: Un juego tipo Space Invaders/Galaxian. Una reminiscencia de juegos electrónicos como Astro Wars y otros. Dispara a los alienígenas antes de que ataquen tu base. Si pasan perderas una vida. ¡Nada más divertido!

Controles: z = izquierda, x = derecha, [espacio]=disparar.

```
10 REM ******ZX Spectrum Code Club *******
15 REM * ASTRAL INVADERS by Gary Plowman *
20 REM *************2015*****************
30 INK 7: PAPER 0: BORDER 0: CLS
45 REM ****** Initialising variables
50 PRINT AT 2,8; INK 7; BRIGHT 1; PAPER 0;"ASTRAL INVADERS":
PRINT AT 4,6;"DONT LET THEM LAND";AT 6,1; INK 6;"Controls:";AT
8,1;"Z=Left, X=Right, Space to fire"
80 PRINT AT 18,5; FLASH 1;"PRESS A KEY TO START": PAUSE 0:
LET hisc=0
100 GO SUB 5000: REM Graphics
110 GO SUB 300: REM initialise
130 GO SUB 1000: REM main loop for game
200 GO TO 30
```

```
 300 REM ***** SETUP
 310 LET lives=5: LET score=0: LET lvl=1: LET ax=INT
(RND*16)+6: LET ay=1: LET alien=145+INT (RND*3): LET acol=INT
(RND*6)+1: LET x=10: LET l$="L E V E L   O N E"
 315 LET speed=.1
 320 RESTORE 340
 305 RANDOMIZE
 390 RETURN
1000 CLS : PRINT AT 0,7;l$: REM ******* MAIN GAME
1010 FOR n = 2 TO 19
1020 PRINT AT n,30; PAPER 6; INK RND*5;CHR$ (137);CHR$
(134);AT n,0;CHR$ (137);CHR$ (134)
1030 NEXT n
1031 FOR n = 16 TO 170
1032 PLOT INK RND*6;INT (RND*200)+20,n
1036 NEXT n
1038 PRINT AT 0,7;"Astral Invaders  "; BRIGHT 1;AT 0,0; INK
2;"1 UP";AT 1,0; INK 7;"0";AT 0,25; INK 2;"Hi-Sc"; INK 7;AT
1,25;hisc
1039 FOR n=1 TO lives: PRINT AT 20,n; INK 6;CHR$ (144): NEXT
n: BEEP 1,4: BRIGHT 1
1040 LET i$=INKEY$()
1060 IF i$="z" THEN LET x=x-1
1070 IF i$="x" THEN LET x=x+1
1080 PRINT AT 18,x;" ";CHR$ (144);" "
1090 IF i$=" " THEN GO SUB 3500: REM Firing
1100 GO SUB 3000: REM Bug movement
1110 IF ay = 19 THEN BEEP .1,2: LET ax=INT (RND*16)+6:
RANDOMIZE : LET lives=lives-1
1120 IF ay=19 THEN FOR n=1 TO lives: PRINT AT 20,n; INK 6;CHR$
(144);" ": NEXT n: LET ay=2
1130 IF lives=0 THEN GO SUB 2000
1300 GO TO 1040
2000 REM ***** DEAD
2010 PRINT AT 18,5; INK 2;"** BASE DESTROYED **"
2020 PRINT AT 10,10; FLASH 1;"PRESS TO RESTART"
```

```
2030 IF INKEY$()="" THEN GO TO 2030
2050 GO TO 100
3000 REM *** move alien
3020 PRINT AT ay,ax;" "
3030 IF ay=9 OR ay=6 THEN LET ax=ax+INT ((RND*2)-(RND*2))
3050 LET ay=ay+1
3060 PRINT AT ay,ax; INK acol;CHR$ (alien): BEEP speed,ay-10
3070 IF score>200 THEN LET l$="L E V E L   T W O"
3080 IF speed > .01 THEN LET speed = speed - .01:
3400 RETURN
3500 REM ***** FIRING
3510 PLOT x*8+12,32: DRAW OVER 1; INK 2;0,100: DRAW OVER 1;0,-
100: PLOT INK 0;x*8+12,132
3520 BEEP .01,10
3530 IF x+1<>ax THEN RETURN
3540 FOR n =7 TO 0 STEP -1
3550 PRINT INK n;AT ay,ax;CHR$ (alien)
3560 BEEP .006,n*2
3570 NEXT n
3575 PRINT AT ay,ax;" "
3580 LET score = score + ((alien-144)*10):
3590 LET ax=INT (RND*16)+6: LET ay=2
3600 IF score> hisc THEN LET hisc=score
3610 PRINT AT 1,0;score;"   ";AT 1,25;hisc;"   "
3620 RANDOMIZE : LET acol=INT (RND*6)+1: LET alien = 145+INT
(RND*3)
3700 RETURN
5000 FOR n = 0 TO 31:
5010 READ dat
5020 POKE USR "a"+n,dat
5030 NEXT n
5050 RETURN
5100 DATA 24,24,189,219,189,165,129,0
5110 DATA 0,24,52,122,60,24,36,66
5120 DATA 60,126,219,219,255,255,153,66
```

```
5130 DATA 36,60,231,102,60,90,24,36
```

¿Qué hay de nuevo?

Hemos configurado y predibujado la pantalla y el movimiento de juego sobrescribe algunos de los fondos, pero no mucho. Esto proporciona una pantalla de juego convincente, bonita y colorida para nuestro disparador.

```
1110 IF ay = 19 THEN BEEP .1,2: LET ax=INT (RND*16)+6:
RANDOMIZE : LET lives=lives-1
```

Arriba podemos ver que perderemos una vida cuando el alienígena llegue al fondo de la pantalla.

```
3000 REM *** move alien
3020 PRINT AT ay,ax;" "
3030 IF ay=9 OR ay=6 THEN LET ax=ax+INT ((RND*2)-(RND*2))
3050 LET ay=ay+1
3060 PRINT AT ay,ax; INK acol;CHR$ (alien): BEEP speed,ay-10
3070 IF score>200 THEN LET l$="L E V E L  T W O"
3080 IF speed > .01 THEN LET speed = speed - .01:
3400 RETURN
```

La sección de arriba controla el movimiento del alienígena y añade un cierto desafío al desplazar el movimiento aleatoriamente a ciertos puntos en la pantalla.

```
3500 REM ***** FIRING
3510 PLOT x*8+12,32: DRAW OVER 1; INK 2;0,100: DRAW OVER 1;0,-
100: PLOT INK 0;x*8+12,132
3520 BEEP .01,10
3530 IF x+1<>ax THEN RETURN
3540 FOR n =7 TO 0 STEP -1
3550 PRINT INK n;AT ay,ax;CHR$ (alien)
3560 BEEP .006,n*2
3570 NEXT n
```

La sección anterior comprobará nuestro disparo. Nuevamente usamos el valor 8* para hacer nuestros comandos PLOT y DRAW y posicionarlos con nuestros UDGs (Sprites).

Recuerda: PLOT coloca el bolígrafo y DRAW dibuja las líneas.

Sugerencias para ampliar el juego (opcional)

1] *Añadir más enemigos al juego*
2] *Añadir más enemigos para que ataquen al jugador al mismo tiempo, dentro de una proximidad cercana en pantalla*
3] *Agregar más efectos de sonido o cambiar los gráficos y la temática de todo el juego a uno de tu preferencia*

COLOUR STACKS

Este es un juego divertido y adictivo, más divertido de lo que su nombre indica. Me encontré con este adictivo puzzle mientras experimentaba con la creación de prototipos de diferentes ideas. Debes evitar los colores incorrectos y ver el contador de movimiento, pero para ello tendrás una cantidad limitada de interruptores que permiten cambiar el color. Planeo publicar una versión móvil de este juego en un futuro próximo.

Jugadores: 1

Reglas: Juego de puzzle en el que el jugador debe unir el bloque al mismo color sin entrar en contacto con ningún otro color. El jugador tiene un contador de movimientos que aumenta si completa las combinaciones correctas.

Controles: q = arriba, a = abajo, o = izquierda, p = derecha, [espacio] = cambiar color.

```
  10 REM ******ZX Spectrum Code Club *******
  15 REM * COLOUR STACKS by Gary Plowman   *
  20 REM *************2015****************
  30 INK 7: PAPER 0: BORDER 4: CLS
  45 REM ****** Initialising variables
  50 PRINT AT 2,10; INK 7; BRIGHT 1; PAPER 0;"COLOUR STACKS":
PRINT AT 4,5;"MATCH COL:OURS TOGETHER!";AT 6,5;"TOUCH A WRONG
COLOUR WILL";AT 8,5;"FORCE A RESTART!";AT 10,5;"[SPACE] to
change colour"
  80 PRINT AT 18,5; FLASH 1;"PRESS A KEY TO START": PAUSE 0
 100 GO SUB 300: REM initialise
 130 GO SUB 1000: REM main loop for game
 200 GO TO 30:
```

```
 300 REM ***** SETUP
 310 LET lives=3: LET score=0: LET misses=0: LET y=19: LET
x=24 : LET timer=50: LET setting=INT (RND*5)+1: LET r=0: LET
xx=0: LET yy=0: LET chg=3:
 320 RANDOMIZE
 390 RETURN
1000 CLS : REM ******* MAIN GAME:
1010 PLOT 10,10: INK 6: DRAW 0,150: DRAW 200,0: DRAW 0,-150:
DRAW -200,0
1020 GO SUB 2000: REM *** DRAW Board
1100 LET i$=INKEY$()
1105 IF timer=0 THEN STOP
1106 PRINT AT 12,27;"Moves";AT 13,27;"Left";AT 15,27;timer;" "
1110 IF i$="" THEN GO TO 1100
1115 LET xx = x: LET yy= y: PRINT AT y,x; PAPER 0;" "
1120 IF i$="o" THEN LET x=x-1
1130 IF i$="p" THEN LET x=x+1
1140 IF i$="q" THEN LET y=y-1
1150 IF i$="a" THEN LET y=y+1
1055 IF x>24 OR x<2 THEN LET x=xx
1056 IF y>19 OR y<2 THEN LET y=yy
1160 IF i$=" " AND chg>0 THEN LET chg=chg-1: BEEP .3,3: LET
setting=INT (RND*5)+1
1170 GO SUB 3000 : REM test for colour
1180 LET timer=timer-1
1200 PRINT AT y,x; INK 7; PAPER setting;"O"
1900 GO TO 1100
2000 FOR n =1 TO 30
2010 PRINT AT INT (RND*13)+3,INT (RND*20)+2; PAPER INT
(RND*5)+1;" "
2030 NEXT n
2040 PRINT AT y,x; INK 7; PAPER setting;"O"
2050 RETURN
3000 REM **** fail if colour doesnt match
3010 LET att1=INT (ATTR (y,x+1)/8)
3020 LET att2=INT (ATTR (y,x-1)/8)
```

```
3030 LET att3=INT (ATTR (y-1,x)/8)
3040 LET att4=INT (ATTR (y+1,x)/8)
3060 IF att1 = setting OR att2=setting OR att3=setting OR
att4=setting THEN PRINT AT y,x; PAPER setting;" ": LET
score=score+setting: LET timer=timer+(setting*2): LET x=xx:
LET y=yy: LET setting=INT (RND*5)+1: BEEP .1,5: RETURN
3070 IF att1 > 0 OR att2>0 OR att3>0 OR att4>0 THEN PRINT
"Dead!": BEEP 1,-5: GO TO 10:ff
3080 PRINT AT 4,27;"SC";AT 6,27;score
3090 PRINT AT 0,2;"You have ";chg;" switches [SP] left"
3100 RETURN
```

¿Qué hay de nuevo?

La función ATTR() es similar a SCREEN$() pero devuelve los atributos de color para la ubicación de pantalla consultada, en forma de valor numérico. Es un poco más complejo pero mucho más útil cuando la detección de colisión no puede transmitir en SCREEN $(). SCREEN $() no funcionará con los UDG, por ejemplo. El funcionamiento de una función ATTR() es más difícil de resolver, pero aquí está la esencia de la misma.

ATTR() es la suma de los siguientes valores de atributos para una sola posición de carácter en la pantalla.

Si la posición del carácter está parpadeando = 128 de otra manera 0
Si la posición del carácter es brillante   = 64 de otra manera 0
Color del papel   = valor de color * 8 (ejemplo Paper Cyan = 5*8 = 40)
Color de la tinta   = valor de color (ejemplo Ink Red = 2)

Agregar todos esos atributos te dirá qué valor debe ser devuelto por la función ATTR(). ATTR es mucho más confiable que SCREEN$().

```
3010 LET att1=INT (ATTR (y,x+1)/8)
```

```
3020 LET att2=INT (ATTR (y,x-1)/8)
3030 LET att3=INT (ATTR (y-1,x)/8)
3040 LET att4=INT (ATTR (y+1,x)/8)
```

3010 a 3040 comprueban todos los lados para la colisión, con colores diferentes a negro y si no coincide con el color, entonces se acaba el juego.

```
1180 LET timer=timer-1
```

Usar un temporizador en el juego es una dinámica buena y fácil y alerta al jugador desde el principio. En este juego usamos el temporizador sólo cuando el jugador se mueve, por lo que no es un temporizador en tiempo real. Debido a que es un puzzle, permitiremos al jugador pensar su siguiente movimiento. Esto también puede ser empleado para un juego donde se reduzca la energía de los jugadores cuando se mueven, obligándoles a comer para recuperarla.

Sugerencias para ampliar el juego (opcional)

1]   Añadir más variaciones al juego (algunos elementos para aumentar el tiempo podrían aparecer al azar)

2]   Añadir pequeñas secciones de laberinto al juego

ANGRY CHICKY

Es el día de Navidad y el joven Timmy tiene hambre a la hora del desayuno, pero necesita huevos para hacer pan y ponche de huevo. El pollo que puso los huevos está enojado y busca morder al pobre Timmy para evitar que coja los huevos. Controla a Timmy para recoger el mayor número de huevos posible y avanza a la siguiente pantalla.

Jugadores: 1

Reglas: Recoge todo el oro y evita las trampas y a los indios apaches.

Controles: q = arriba, a = abajo, o = izquierda, p = derecha. También servirá un Joystick si se dispone de uno..

Bono: Como tarea en el apartado gráfico, trata de calcular el BIN a los valores decimales para los gráficos, para no tener que teclear 1s y 0s.

```
10 REM *********ZX Spectrum Code Club *********
15 REM * ANGRY CHICKY by G Plowman 2015        *
20 REM ****************************************
25 GO SUB 7000: REM **** Create graphics
30 INK 1: PAPER 7: BORDER 4: CLS
45 REM ****** Initialising variables
50 PRINT AT 2,10; INK 7; BRIGHT 1; PAPER 2;"ANGRY CHICKY":
PRINT AT 4,5;"Help Timmy ";CHR$ (145);" grab eggs to
make his Eggy Bread";AT 6,5;"Avoid the Angry Chicky!!"; INK
2;CHR$ (146)
35 LET lives=3
60 PRINT AT 7,5;"Avoid the cracked ice!"; PAPER 5; INK 2;"x"
65 PRINT AT 8,5;"Collect the EGGS!"; PAPER 6;"o"
```

```
  70 PRINT AT 11,2;"Controls: ";AT 12,2;"Q/A=Up/Down,
O/P=Left/Right"
  80 PRINT AT 18,5; FLASH 1;"PRESS A KEY TO START": PAUSE 0
 100 GO SUB 300: REM initialise
 130 GO SUB 1000: REM main loop for game
 200 GO TO 30
 300 REM ***** SETUP
 310 LET x=10: LET y=10: LET vx=0: LET vy=0: LET score=0: LET
lvl=1: LET ax=1: LET ay=1: LET ax2=0: LET ay2=0: LET loot=0
 330 RETURN
1000 CLS
1010 FOR n = 0 TO 19:
1030 PRINT AT n,0;CHR$ (144);AT n,31;CHR$ (144)
1040 NEXT n
1045 FOR n=1 TO 30
1050 PRINT AT 0,n;CHR$ (144);AT 19,n;CHR$ (144)
1060 NEXT n
1070 FOR n = 1 TO 20
1080 PRINT AT INT (RND*15)+3,INT (RND*25)+3; PAPER 5; INK
2;"x"
1085 NEXT n
1086 FOR n = 1 TO 5
1087 PRINT AT INT (RND*15)+3,INT (RND*25)+3; PAPER 6;"o"
1090 NEXT n
1095 PRINT AT 20,1;"Eggy Bread: ";score
1100 LET i$=INKEY$(): LET i=IN 31
1110 IF (i$="q" OR i=8) AND y>2 THEN LET vy=-1: LET vx=0
1120 IF (i$="a" OR i=4) AND y<19 THEN LET vy=1: LET vx=0
1130 IF (i$="o" OR i=2) AND x>2 THEN LET vx=-1: LET vy=0
1140 IF (i$="p" OR i=1) AND y<30 THEN LET vx=1: LET vy=0
1145 LET x=x+vx: LET y  =y+vy
1150 IF x=0 THEN GO SUB 2000
1160 IF x=31 THEN GO SUB 2000
1170 IF y=19 THEN GO SUB 2000
1180 IF y=0 THEN GO SUB 2000
1185 LET a$=SCREEN$ (y,x)
```

```
1190 IF a$="x" OR (y=ay AND x=ax) THEN GO SUB 2000
1200 IF a$="o" THEN GO SUB 3000
1210 PRINT AT y,x;CHR$ (145)
1230 IF vx<>0 THEN PRINT AT y,x-vx;" "
1240 IF vy<>0 THEN PRINT AT y-vy,x;" "
1250 IF lvl>0 THEN GO SUB 3500
1300 GO TO 1100
1900 STOP
2000 PRINT AT 21,15;"DEAD!";AT 15,10; FLASH 1;"RESTARTING":
BEEP 2,1: PAUSE 1000
2100 GO TO 30
3000 REM *** * Collect loot
3010 LET score = score +(INT (RND*4)+1)
3020 PRINT AT 20,1; PAPER 6; INK 2;"Eggy Bread: ";score: BEEP
.05,20
3030 LET loot=loot+1
3040 IF loot=5 THEN PRINT AT 15,10; FLASH 1;"NEXT ROUND!":
BEEP 2,1
3050 IF loot=5 THEN LET loot=0: LET lvl=lvl+1: LET ax=2: LET
ay=2: LET vx=0: LET vy=0: GO TO 1000
3060 RETURN
3500 REM **** Move Chicky
3505 LET ax2=ax: LET ay2=ay
3510 IF ax>x THEN PRINT AT ay,ax;" ": LET ax=ax-1: GO TO 3550:
3520 IF ax<x THEN PRINT AT ay,ax;" ": LET ax=ax+1: GO TO 3550
3530 IF ay<y THEN PRINT AT ay,ax;" ": LET ay=ay+1.2: GO TO
3550
3540 IF ay>y THEN PRINT AT ay,ax;" ": LET ay=ay-1.2
3550 IF SCREEN$ (ay,ax)<>" " THEN LET ax=ax2: LET ay=ay2:
3560 PRINT AT ay,ax; INK 2;CHR$ (146):
3565 IF ax=x AND ABS (ay-y)<1.5 THEN GO TO 2000
3590 RETURN
7000 FOR n = 0 TO 23
7010 READ dat
7020 POKE USR "a"+n,dat
7030 NEXT n
```

```
7040 RETURN
7050 DATA BIN 00111100
7060 DATA BIN 01000011
7070 DATA BIN 10110101
7080 DATA BIN 11000011
7090 DATA BIN 10000001
7110 DATA BIN 10000001
7120 DATA BIN 01000010
7130 DATA BIN 00111100
7150 DATA BIN 00111100
7160 DATA BIN 01111000
7165 DATA BIN 01100111
7170 DATA BIN 00100100
7180 DATA BIN 10111101
7210 DATA BIN 11111111
7220 DATA BIN 11000011
7230 DATA BIN 00000000
7350 DATA BIN 00111000
7360 DATA BIN 00110110
7365 DATA BIN 01111111
7370 DATA BIN 11100101
7380 DATA BIN 11011000
7410 DATA BIN 10111110
7420 DATA BIN 01111111
7430 DATA BIN 00111100
```

Temas divertidos

Un juego divertido con una premisa divertida. Eso es lo que muchos de los clásicos del Spectrum tienen en común. Juegos como Mathew Smith Manic Miner y Jet Set Willy. La escena británica está literalmente llena de juegos que se basaban en ideas extravagantes. No tengas miedo de experimentar y divertirte mientras haces tus juegos.

¿Qué hay de nuevo?

Hemos utilizado la función ABS() en nuestro código, la cual es útil para calcular distancias de objetos entre sí, entre otras muchas cosas. Esta función devuelve el resultado como un valor absoluto, por ejemplo, lo convierte en positivo. Así que -1 se convierte en 1 y +1 es 1. Esto te permite probar la diferencia entre dos valores sin necesidad de preocuparte si el valor probado es +2 o -2. El caso en Angry Chicky es descubrir si Chicky ha atrapado a Timmy.

Sugerencias para ampliar el juego (opcional)

1]   *Añadir otro Angry Chicky para perseguir al jugador*
2]   *Añadir más elementos para recopilar*
3]   *Añadir una puntuación de bonificación al temporizador*
     para animar al usuario a completar la pantalla más rápido

ALLOTMENT WARS

En este extraño juego tienes que ganar dinero con tus productos y competir contra otros distribuidores de vegetales, mientras se sabotean el uno al otro. ¡Lanza vegetales dañados en el huerto de tus oponentes para reducir su oferta! Este juego es un ejemplo de los locos días de programación de dormitorio que hicieron grande a la escena británica. Este juego no entra en esa liga, pero no desprecies las ideas raras de inmediato. Algunos juegos indie muy exitosos suenan terrible cuando apenas son una idea. Este juego está hecho para extender o cambiar, así que puedes desarmarlo y añadir características adicionales, etc.

Jugadores: 1

Reglas: Arroja vegetales dañados para golpear los vegetales de tus oponentes. Cada disparo que realices, permite que tus oponentes te disparen. Pierde quien tenga puntaje inferior a -4 y gana la ronda quien tenga puntaje de 5 o más.

Controles: Se ubica al jardinero con las teclas de la A a la G o de 1 a 7. A = Cruza, U = Arriba, D = Diagonal

```
  10 REM ********************************
  20 REM * ALLOTMENT WARS - Gary Plowman   *
  25 REM ********************************
  30 INK 7: PAPER 0: BORDER 0
  45 GO SUB 5000
  50 CLS : PRINT AT 2,10; INK 6; BRIGHT 1; PAPER 1;"ALLOTMENT
WARS": LET lvl = 10: LET round=1
  60 PRINT AT 4,1;"You must win Best Allotment"
  70 PRINT AT 6,1;"Throw weeds to spoil opp. Veg  "
  75 PRINT AT 8,1;"Score 5 to get to next round!";AT
10,1;"Each Veg you hit will give you an extra Veg"
```

```
  80 PRINT AT 18,5; FLASH 1;"PRESS A KEY TO START": PAUSE 0:
CLS : RANDOMIZE
 110 GO SUB 300: REM initialise
 130 GO SUB 1000: REM draw screen
 140 GO SUB 3000: REM draw info on screen
 150 GO SUB 2000: main loop
 160 GO TO 50
 300 REM **** Setup
 310 LET score1=0: DIM v(3): LET score2=0: LET score3=0: LET
score4=0
 320 LET power=0: LET rightpos=0: LET toppos=0: LET g$="CPBT":
LET targ=0: LET turn=1
 400 RETURN
1000 REM **** Screen
1005 PRINT AT 1,23;"ALLOTMENT";AT 2,25;"WARS"
1010 FOR n=1 TO 7
1020 PRINT AT n,5; PAPER 4;"-*-*-*-";
1030 PRINT AT n+10,5; PAPER 4;"-*-*-*-"; PAPER 0;n
1040 PRINT AT n,15; PAPER 4;"-*-*-*-";
1050 PRINT AT n+10,15; PAPER 4;"-*-*-*-";
1080 NEXT n
1085 RANDOMIZE
1090 PRINT AT 7,12; INK 3;CHR$ (144);AT 7,14; INK 5;CHR$
(144);AT 10,20; INK 2;CHR$ (144)
1100 PRINT AT 10,5;"ABCDEFG";AT 19,0;"GROWING VEG - PLEASE
WAIT..."
1120 PRINT AT 9,13; INK 6;CHR$ (144)
1140 REM ******* WE ADD SOME VEG
1150 FOR n = 1 TO 18
1160 FOR m = 1 TO 20
1165 LET rn =INT (RND*lvl)+1
1170 IF SCREEN$ (n,m)="*" AND rn<5 THEN PRINT AT n,m; PAPER 4;
INK 3;g$(rn)
1180 NEXT m
1190 NEXT n
1500 RETURN
```

```
2000 REM **** Main Loop
2010 LET a$=INKEY$()
2020 IF a$="" THEN GO TO 2010
2030 IF a$>="1" AND a$<="7" THEN LET rightpos = VAL a$: GO SUB
2500: GO SUB 3000
2040 IF a$>="a" AND a$<="g" THEN LET toppos = CODE a$-96: GO
SUB 2500: GO SUB 3000
2100 GO TO 2010
2500 REM **** Throw weeds
2505 PRINT AT 10,13;" ": BEEP .05,4
2510 IF rightpos>0 THEN PRINT AT 10+rightpos,13; INK 6;CHR$
(144): PRINT AT 10,13;" "
2515 IF toppos>0 THEN PRINT AT 9,4+toppos; INK 6;CHR$ (144):
PRINT AT 10,13;" "
2520 PRINT AT 19,0;"Fire (A)cross (U)p or (D)iagonal";AT
9,13;" "
2540 LET power=power+1: PRINT AT  20,0;"Pwr:"
2550 LET b$=INKEY$()
2560 PRINT INK 2;AT 20,3+power;" ";CHR$ (138)
2570 IF power > 8 THEN LET power = 1
2580 IF b$="a" OR b$="u" OR b$="d" THEN GO TO 2600
2590 GO TO 2540:
2600 BEEP .05,4: LET fx=0: LET fy=0
2610 FOR n = power TO 1 STEP -.5
2620 BEEP .05,n
2630 NEXT n
2650 IF rightpos>0 AND b$="a" THEN LET fx= 13+power: LET
fy=10+rightpos
2660 IF rightpos>0 AND b$="u" THEN LET fx=13: LET
fy=10+rightpos-power
2670 IF rightpos>0 AND b$="d" THEN LET fx=13+power: LET
fy=10+rightpos-power
2680 IF toppos>0 AND b$="a" THEN LET fx=4+toppos+power: LET
fy=9
2690 IF toppos>0 AND b$="u" THEN LET fx=4+toppos: LET fy=9-
power
```

```
2700 IF toppos>0 AND b$="d" THEN LET fx=4+toppos+power: LET
fy=9-power
2710 LET r$=SCREEN$ (fy,fx)
2710 PRINT AT fy,fx; INK 6;"."
2715 IF fx<12 THEN LET targ=1
2720 IF fx>12 AND fy<9 THEN LET targ=2
2730 IF fx>12 AND fy>9 THEN LET targ=3:
2735 LET rightpos=0: LET toppos=0
2740 IF r$="C" OR r$="P" OR r$="B" OR r$="T" THEN LET
score1=score1+1: BEEP .5,9: LET vgx=5: LET vgy=11: GO SUB 3200
2745 GO SUB 3300
2750 RETURN
3000 REM **** Redraw INFO *******
3010 PRINT AT 9,5;"           "
3020 FOR n = 1 TO 9
3030 PRINT AT 8+n,13;" "
3040 NEXT n
3050 PRINT AT 19,0;"Select A - G or 1 - 7          ";AT
20,0;"                    "
3060 PRINT AT 3,23; INK 6;"You: ";CHR$ (96);score1;" ";AT
4,23; INK 3;"Purp:";CHR$ (96);v(1);" ";AT 5,23; INK
5;"Blue:";CHR$ (96);v(2);" ";AT 6,23; INK 2;"Red: ";CHR$
(96);v(3);" ";
3070 PRINT AT 9,13; INK 6;CHR$ (144)
3075 PRINT AT 8,23;"ROUND:";round
3080 IF score1<-2 OR score1>4 THEN GO SUB 3400:
3090 RETURN
3200 REM **** WIN SOME VEG
3201 LET cnt=0
3205 IF targ> 0 THEN LET v(targ)=v(targ)-1
3206 IF targ=0 THEN LET v(turn)=v(turn)+1
3210 LET vegx=vegx+INT (RND*8): LET vegy=vegy+INT (RND*8): REM
LET vg =INT (RND*4)+1
3220 IF SCREEN$ (vegy,vegx)="*" THEN PRINT AT vegy,vegx; PAPER
4; INK 1;r$: RETURN
3225 LET cnt = cnt + 1
```

```
3226 IF cnt > 40 THEN RETURN
3230 GO TO 3210
3240 RETURN
3300 REM *** Enemy shoot
3304 BEEP .4,3: PRINT AT 19,0;"Opponents throws weed!
"
3310 FOR n = 10 TO 1 STEP -1: BEEP .06,n: NEXT n:
3315 LET fx = 5+INT (RND*7): LET fy=11+INT (RND*7):
3320 IF turn=1 THEN LET vgx =5 : LET vgy =1
3330 IF turn=2 THEN LET vgx =15 : LET vgy =1
3340 IF turn=3 THEN LET vgx =15 : LET vgy =11
3350 LET r$=SCREEN$ (fy,fx)
3360 PRINT AT fy,fx; INK 6;"."
3370 IF r$="C" OR r$="P" OR r$="B" OR r$="T" THEN LET
score1=score1-1: LET targ=0: BEEP .5,9: GO SUB 3200
3380 LET turn=turn+1
3385 IF turn>3 THEN LET turn=1
3390 RETURN
3400 REM WIN OR LOSE
3410 IF score1 < -2 THEN PRINT AT 10,10; FLASH 1;"UH! OH! YOU
LOSE!": BEEP 1,0: PAUSE 0: GO TO 50
3420 IF score1> 4 THEN PRINT AT 10,10; FLASH 1;"NEXT ROUND!":
LET round = round + 1: LET lvl = lvl +3: BEEP 1,10: PAUSE 0:
CLS : GO TO 110
3430 IF lvl>25 THEN LET lvl = 25:
5000 FOR n = 0 TO 7
5010 READ dat
5020 POKE USR "a"+n,dat
5030 NEXT n
5040 RETURN
5050 DATA 24,126,24,24,10,60,56,8
```

¿Qué hay de nuevo?

El concepto original de este juego cambió unas cuantas veces. Al final pasé de un juego de acción a uno basado en turnos. Esto fue ocasionado por los límites del Spectrum y a su modo de juego. Este juego ofrece más opciones de extensión que la versión arcade. Si lo deseas, puedes volver a escribirlo o convertirlo en un juego multijugador (hotseat) de 1 a 4 jugadores y los jugadores restantes son controlados por la CPU.

Reducción de código

Hemos sido capaces de reducir el número de sentencias IF para pulsaciones de teclas mediante el uso de código que traduce la información de pulsaciones de teclas, en coordenadas para nuestro juego.

```
2030 IF a$>="1" AND a$<="7" THEN LET rightpos = VAL a$: GO SUB
2500: GO SUB 3000
2040 IF a$>="a" AND a$<="g" THEN LET toppos = CODE a$-96: GO
SUB 2500: GO SUB 3000
```

VAL convierte números de cadena a números reales y CODE devuelve el valor de conjunto de caracteres para un carácter de cadena.

Sugerencias para ampliar el juego (opcional)

1] Añadir más funciones. Ejemplo: Multijugador
2] Hacer que el tipo de vegetal cuente. Ejemplo, dar puntuación diferente por cada tipo de vegetal.
3] Agregar eventos aleatorios que afecten el juego

RETRO HUNTER

Little Ally ha ido a una expo de juegos retro y debe tratar de recoger tantos juegos como pueda dentro del límite de tiempo. Se mueve como loco y corre en una dirección hasta que llega a un stand o la pared del edificio. Cuantos más juegos recoja, más tiempo se añadirá a su temporizador. Sin embargo, hay otros Coleccionistas Retro que también quieren juegos retro. Por lo tanto tienes que moverte rápido por la Expo, en este pequeño pero divertido juego de puzzle.

Jugadores: 2

Reglas: Caminar por la ubicación y usar los puestos para llegar a las áreas donde podrás recoger los juegos.

Controles: q = arriba, a = abajo, o = izquierda, p = derecho para mover.

```
  10 REM ******ZX Spectrum Code Club *******
  15 REM * RETRO HUNTER by Gary Plowman   *
  20 REM *************2015*****************
  30 INK 0: PAPER 5: BORDER 1: CLS
  40 GO SUB 6000
  50 PRINT AT 2,10; INK 7; BRIGHT 1; PAPER 0;"RETRO HUNTER"
  60 PRINT AT 4,5;"Collect games to succeed!";AT
5,5;"Collections increase Timer!"
  80 PRINT AT 18,5; FLASH 1;"PRESS A KEY TO START": PAUSE 0:
CLS : RANDOMIZE
 110 GO SUB 300: REM initialise:
 130 GO SUB 1000: REM draw screen
 140 GO SUB 2000: REM main loop
 300 REM *******
```

```
 310 LET x= 7: LET y=17: LET vy=0: LET vx=0: LET sega=0: LET
nin=0: LET spec=0: LET comm=0: LET timer=100
 400 RETURN
1000 REM ****** Screen
1010 CLS : INK 5: PAPER 5: PRINT INK 0;AT 0,4;"RUN AROUND PLAY
EXPO HALL";AT 1,4;"COLLECTING RETRO GAMES!" ;AT 20,0;"*RETRO
HUNTER*"
1020 PRINT AT 03,5;"MMMMMMMMMMMM"
1030 PRINT AT 04,5;"MM          MM"
1040 PRINT AT 05,5;"M  M  M     M"
1050 PRINT AT 06,5;"M    M  MMM  M"
1060 PRINT AT 07,5;"MM       M    M"
1070 PRINT AT 08,5;"M    M      MM"
1080 PRINT AT 09,5;"M  MMMM M    M"
1090 PRINT AT 10,5;"M       M    M"
1100 PRINT AT 11,5;"MMM         M"
1110 PRINT AT 12,5;"M           M"
1120 PRINT AT 13,5;"M          MMM"
1130 PRINT AT 14,5;"MM   M  M   M"
1140 PRINT AT 15,5;"M    MM     M"
1145 PRINT AT 16,5;"M  MMM      M"
1140 PRINT AT 17,5;"M         M  M"
1150 PRINT AT 18,5;"MMMMMMMMMMMM"
1160 FOR n=3 TO 18
1170 FOR m = 5 TO 18
1180 IF SCREEN$ (n,m)="M" THEN PRINT AT n,m; PAPER 1; INK
1;;"M"
1190 NEXT m: NEXT n
1200 INK 2: PRINT AT 3,20;"SEGA: ";sega;AT 5,20;"Nndo:
";nin;AT 7,20;"ZXSp: ";spec;AT 9,20;"C-64: ";comm
1210 LET score= nin+spec+sega+comm
1220 IF score<10 THEN LET s$="Novice"
1230 IF score>=10 THEN LET s$="Beginner"
1240 IF score>30 THEN LET s$="RetroFan"
1250 IF score>50 THEN LET s$="RetroGuru!"
1280 PRINT AT 18,20;s$;" "
```

```
1300 RETURN
2000 REM GAME LOOP
2010 LET i$=INKEY$(): LET j=IN 31
2110 IF (i$="q" OR j=8) AND (vx=0 AND vy=0) THEN LET vy=-1:
LET vx=0
2120 IF (i$="a" OR j=4) AND (vx=0 AND vy=0) THEN LET vy=1: LET
vx=0
2140 IF (i$="o" OR j=1) AND (vx=0 AND vy=0) THEN LET vx=-1:
LET vy=0
2130 IF (i$="p" OR j=2) AND (vx=0 AND vy=0) THEN LET vx=1: LET
vy=0
2190 IF SCREEN$ (y+vy,x+vx)<>"M" THEN PRINT AT y,x;" ": LET
x=x+vx: LET y=y+vy
2192 IF SCREEN$ (y+vy,x+vx)="M" THEN LET vx=0: LET vy=0
2195 LET y$=SCREEN$ (y,x)
2200 IF y$="S" THEN LET sega = sega +1: LET timer=timer+20:
BEEP .2,8: GO SUB 1200
2210 IF y$="C" THEN LET comm = comm+1: LET timer=timer+10:
BEEP .2,5: GO SUB 1200
2220 IF y$="Z" THEN LET spec = spec +1: LET timer=timer+30:
BEEP .2,13: GO SUB 1200
2230 IF y$="N" THEN LET nin = nin +1: LET timer=timer+20: BEEP
.2,8: GO SUB 1200
2240 IF timer> 160 THEN LET timer=160:
2290 PRINT AT y,x; INK 0;CHR$ (144);AT 20,20;"Clock:";timer;"
"
2300 LET timer=timer-1
2310 IF timer <= 0 THEN PRINT AT 10,10;"GAME OVER";AT
12,10;"SCORE WAS ";score: BEEP 2,10: CLS : GO TO 50
2400 IF INT (RND*100)<6 THEN GO SUB 3100
2410 IF INT (RND*50)<20 THEN GO SUB 3200
3000 GO TO 2000
3100 REM ***** PLACE COLLECTABLE
3110 LET cx=6+INT (RND*10): LET cy=4+INT (RND*10): LET ty=INT
(RND*4)+1
3120 IF SCREEN$ (cy,cx)="M" THEN GO TO 3110
```

```
3130 IF ty=1 THEN LET t$="S"
3140 IF ty=2 THEN LET t$="N"
3150 IF ty=3 THEN LET t$="C"
3160 IF ty=4 THEN LET t$="Z":
3170 PRINT AT cy,cx; INK ty-1;t$:
3190 RETURN
3200 REM ***** MOVE OTHER COLLECTORS
3210 LET cx=6+INT (RND*10): LET cy=4+INT (RND*10)
3220 LET c$=SCREEN$ (cy,cx)
3230 IF c$="S" OR c$="Z" OR c$="N" OR c$="C" THEN PRINT AT
cy,cx; INK 2;CHR$ (144): BEEP .3,-3:
3250 RETURN
6000 FOR n = 0 TO 7
6010 READ dat
6020 POKE USR "a"+n,dat
6030 NEXT n
6040 RETURN
6100 DATA  8,20,95,62,62,28,20,20
```

Juegos de Puzzle

Este tipo de juegos funciona muy bien en Sinclair BASIC. Por lo general, no dependen de la acción rápida sino de pensamiento y análisis. Se puede cambiar este juego de muchas maneras y hacer que tenga otra temática que sea de interés para ti o para alguien más. Se puede cambiar el nivel de la pantalla alterando las líneas 1020 a 1150. De igual manera, sólo se requieren algunos cambios para hacer un juego de laberinto sencillo, a partir de este código base.

```
1020 PRINT AT 03,5;"MMMMMMMMMMMMM"
1030 PRINT AT 04,5;"MM          MM"
1040 PRINT AT 05,5;"M  M  M      M"
1050 PRINT AT 06,5;"M    M  MMM   M"
1060 PRINT AT 07,5;"MM        M    M"
```

```
1070 PRINT AT 08,5;"M    M        MM"
1080 PRINT AT 09,5;"M  MMMM M    M"
1090 PRINT AT 10,5;"M       M      M"
1100 PRINT AT 11,5;"MMM          M"
1110 PRINT AT 12,5;"M            M"
1120 PRINT AT 13,5;"M          MMM"
1130 PRINT AT 14,5;"MM    M  M    M"
1140 PRINT AT 15,5;"M    MM      M"
1145 PRINT AT 16,5;"M   MMM      M"
1140 PRINT AT 17,5;"M         M   M"
1150 PRINT AT 18,5;"MMMMMMMMMMMM"
```

Hacer el juego divertido

Todo el mundo quiere hacer un juego divertido, pero el concepto puede sonar mucho más divertido que el resultado final. El juego Retro Hunter comenzó con el personaje de Ally recopilando los juegos en contra del reloj, pero no representaba ningún reto más que un juego de laberinto. La versión final se convirtió en un juego de puzzle, con tan sólo hacer pequeños ajustes al código y un rediseño del mapa de la pantalla. Así que volver a pensar las ideas es mejor que desechar el juego completo. ¡Y ahora es mucho más divertido!

Sugerencias para ampliar el juego (opcional)

1] Diseñar mapa y temática propia usando la misma mecánica
2] Aumentar el tamaño de la pantalla
3] Añadir un modo de 2 jugadores, quienes jugarán por turnos

SNOWBALL SHOOTOUT

Ninguna lista de juegos está completa sin un juego de temática navideña. Trata de vencer al otro equipo al anotar 5 bolas de nieve antes que ellos. Elige al tirador de tu equipo y a dos miembros para ocultarse.

Jugadores: 2

Reglas: Elige a un tirador y a dos de tu equipo para ocultarse. Se precavido y no dejes ver tus pulsaciones de teclas a tus oponentes.

Controles: Teclas 1 a 4.

```
  10 REM ******** ZX Spectrum Code Club *********
  15 REM * SNOWBALL SHOOTOUT by G Plowman 2015  *
  18 REM *****************************************
  20 BRIGHT 1: INK 2: PAPER 7: BORDER 4 : CLS
  30 GO SUB 5000: REM *** graphics
  40 GO SUB 200: REM *** Setup
  50 GO SUB 300: REM *** Restart
  60 GO SUB 1000: REM *** Main loop:
 200 LET score=0: DIM p(4): DIM o(4): LET turn=1: LET
shoot1=0: LET shoot2=0: LET sc1=0: LET sc2=0: LET hide=0
 210 FOR n = 1 TO 4
 220 LET p(n)=0: LET o(n)=0
 250 RETURN
 300 PRINT AT 6,5;"Snowball Shootout!"
 310 PRINT AT 8,5;"Winter Is Coming!";AT 10,5;"EACH TURN:";AT
12,5;"Choose your player to shoot";AT 16,3; FLASH 1;"PRESS A
KEY TO START":
 320 BEEP 1,4: PAUSE 0: CLS
```

```
 390 RETURN
1000 REM *** Main loop / Setup screen
1005 LET hide=0
1010 FOR n =1 TO 20 STEP 2
1020 PRINT INK 4;AT n,0;CHR$ (146);AT n,30;CHR$ (146)
1030 PRINT INK 4;AT n+1,0;CHR$ (147);AT n+1,30;CHR$ (147)
1040 NEXT n:
1050 FOR n = 0 TO 30
1060 PRINT INK 4;AT 0,n;CHR$ (147);AT 20,n;CHR$ (146)
1070 NEXT n:
1110 PRINT AT 3,7;"                    ";AT 4,7;"
"
1112 PRINT AT 17,7;"                    ";AT 18,7;"
"
1115 FOR n =1 TO 4
1120 PRINT INK 4;AT 4,6+n*3;CHR$ (146);AT 16,6+n*3;CHR$
(146);" "
1130 PRINT INK 4;AT 5,6+n*3;CHR$ (147);AT 17,6+n*3;CHR$
(147);" ":
1140 NEXT n
1150 FOR n = 1 TO 4
1155 IF p(n)=10 THEN GO TO 1165
1160 PRINT INK n+1;AT 3,7+n*3;CHR$ (145)
1165 IF o(n)=10 THEN GO TO 1185
1170 PRINT INK n;AT 18,7+n*3;CHR$ (145)
1185 NEXT n:
1190 PRINT AT 10,5; INK 1; PAPER 4;"BEGIN SNOWFIGHT!": PAUSE
0: GO SUB 3000: REM clear part of screen
1200 REM *** game loop
1205 LET hide=0
1210 IF turn=1 THEN PRINT AT 10,5; INK 1; PAPER 4;"PLAYER 1:
";AT 11,5;"PRESS 1-4 FOR :shooter ";AT 3,2; PAPER 7;"PLY 2";AT
18,2; PAPER 4;"PLY 1"
1212 IF turn=2 THEN PRINT AT 10,5; INK 1; PAPER 4;"PLAYER 2:
";AT 11,5;"PRESS 1-4 FOR :shooter ";AT 18,2; PAPER 7;"PLY
1";AT 3,2; PAPER 4;"PLY 2";
```

```
1215 PRINT AT 3,26;"SC:";AT 4,26;sc2;;AT 18,26;"SC:";AT
19,26;sc1
1220 LET i$=INKEY$(): LET v=0
1225 IF i$>="1" AND i$<="4" THEN LET v=VAL i$: GO TO 1240
1230 GO TO 1220
1240 IF v<1 AND v>4 THEN BEEP .4,0: REM ** wrong!
1250 IF p(v)<11 AND turn=1 THEN BEEP .1,12: LET p(v)=1: GO TO
1280
1260 IF o(v)<11 AND turn=2 THEN BEEP .1,12: LET o(v)=1: GO TO
1280
1270 GO TO 1220:
1280 LET i$=INKEY$(): LET v=0: REM ** Select who is to take
cover
1285 IF i$>="1" AND i$<="4" THEN LET v=VAL i$
1290 IF turn=1 THEN PRINT AT 10,5; INK 1; PAPER 4;"PLAYER 1:
";AT 11,5;"PRESS 1-4 to Take Cover"
1290 IF turn=2 THEN PRINT AT 10,5; INK 1; PAPER 4;"PLAYER 2:
";AT 11,5;"PRESS 1-4 to Take Cover"
1295 IF v=0 THEN GO TO 1280
1300 IF v>=1 AND v<=4 AND turn=1 AND p(v)<10 THEN GO TO 1360
1310 IF v>=1 AND v<=4 AND turn=2 AND o(v)<10 THEN GO TO 1350
1330 GO TO 1280:
1350 IF o(v)=0 AND turn=2 THEN BEEP .1,8: LET o(v)=2: LET
hide=hide+1
1360 IF p(v)=0 AND turn=1 THEN BEEP .1,8: LET p(v)=2: LET
hide=hide+1
1370 GO SUB 3400
1390 IF turn=1 AND (check1=5) AND hide=2 THEN LET turn=2: GO
TO 1200
1400 IF turn=2 AND (check2=5) AND hide=2 THEN BEEP .4,4: GO
SUB 3000: GO SUB 2000:
1450 GO TO 1280
1600 REM *** Redraw Teams:
1610 FOR n=1 TO 4
1620 IF p(n)=1 THEN PRINT AT 18,7+n*3;" ";AT 17,7+n*3; INK
n;CHR$ (145)
```

```
1630 IF o(n)=1 THEN PRINT AT 3,7+n*3;" ";AT 4,7+n*3; INK
n+1;CHR$ (145)
1640 IF p(n)=0 THEN PRINT AT 18,7+n*3;" ";AT 17,7+n*3;" ";AT
18,7+n*3; INK n;CHR$ (145)
1650 IF o(n)=0 THEN PRINT AT 3,7+n*3;" ";AT 4,7+n*3;" ";AT
3,7+n*3; INK n;CHR$ (145)
1660 IF p(n)=2 THEN PRINT AT 18,7+n*3;" ";AT 18,6+n*3; INK
n+1;CHR$ (145)
1670 IF o(n)=2 THEN PRINT AT 3,7+n*3;" ";AT 3,6+n*3; INK
n;CHR$ (145)
1690 NEXT n
1700 RETURN
2000 REM *** NEXT Turn
2010 GO SUB 1600
2020 FOR n = 1 TO 4
2030 IF p(n)=1 THEN LET shoot1=n
2040 IF o(n)=1 THEN LET shoot2=n
2050 NEXT n
2060 REM *** shoot
2070 FOR n = 1 TO 13
2080 PRINT AT 16-n+1,7+shoot1*3;" ":
2090 PRINT AT 5+n-1,7+shoot2*3;" "
2100 PRINT AT 16-n,7+shoot1*3;CHR$ (144)
2110 PRINT AT 5+n,7+shoot2*3;CHR$ (144)
2120 BEEP .1,n
2140 NEXT n
2150 IF o(shoot1)<2 THEN BEEP 1,12: PRINT AT
3,7+shoot1*3;"ow!": LET o(shoot1)=10: LET sc1=sc1+1
2150 IF p(shoot2)<2 THEN BEEP 1,12: PRINT AT
18,7+shoot2*3;"ow!": LET p(shoot2)=10: LET sc2=sc2+1
2200 LET turn = 1
2210 REM PRINT AT 11,3;"NEXT ROUND!!":
2220 FOR n=1 TO 4
2230 IF o(n)<11 THEN LET o(n)=0
2240 IF p(n)<11 THEN LET p(n)=0
2250 NEXT n
```

```
2260 GO SUB 3400: REM ** check team
2270 IF sc2>=5 AND sc1<sc2 THEN PRINT AT 10,10;"PLAYER 1
LOST!": PAUSE 100: BEEP 1,10: PAUSE 0: CLS : GO TO 40
2280 IF sc1>=5 AND sc2<sc1 THEN PRINT AT 10,10;"PLAYER 2
LOST!": PAUSE 100: BEEP 1,10: PAUSE 0: CLS : GO TO 40
2290 GO TO 1110
2300 RETURN
3000 REM *** Clear screen routine
3010 PRINT AT 10,3;"                          "
3020 PRINT AT 11,3;"                          "
3030 RETURN
3400 REM *** Checking teams routine
3410 LET check1=p(1)+p(2)+p(3)+p(4)
3420 LET check2=o(1)+o(2)+o(3)+o(4)
3450 RETURN
5000 FOR n = 0 TO 31:
5010 READ dat
5020 POKE USR "a"+n,dat
5030 NEXT n
5050 RETURN
5100 DATA 0,24,52,122,60,24,0,0
5110 DATA 24,60,102,102,60,219,24,36
5120 DATA 8,28,28,42,73,28,42,73
5130 DATA 28,42,73,28,42,73,28,62
```

Progreso

Si has llegado hasta aquí tu nivel de BASIC ha avanzado y has aprendido intuitivamente lo que hacen la mayoría de comandos BASIC. También debes estar familiarizado con la programación en una plantilla simple para un juego nuevo.

¡Así fue que yo aprendí a programar!

¿Qué hay de nuevo?

Los loops son muy prácticos para hacer un trabajo grande con muy poco código. Una manera fácil de pensar en ello es "contar del 1 al 13". El código FOR 'n=x a y' y el código NEXT n son el punto inicial y final del loop y se repite trece veces. Otros idiomas tienen otros tipos de loops, pero el loop FOR NEXT fue creado originalmente en Sinclair BASIC.

```
2070 FOR n = 1 TO 13
2080 PRINT AT 16-n+1,7+shoot1*3;" ":
2090 PRINT AT 5+n-1,7+shoot2*3;" "
2100 PRINT AT 16-n,7+shoot1*3;CHR$ (144)
2110 PRINT AT 5+n,7+shoot2*3;CHR$ (144)
2120 BEEP .1,n
2140 NEXT n
```

El código anterior crea el efecto de disparo en el juego. También puede contar hacia atrás, proporcionando algo para usar como...

```
2070 FOR n = 13 TO 1 STEP -1
```

Si el loop es pequeño no es la mejor opción. Normalmente no se loopea de 1 a 2. Ten en cuenta los comandos que tienes dentro de tu loop. Los comandos lentos pueden ralentizar significativamente tu código, si están incluidos sin razón aparente o por error en un loop.

Sugerencias para ampliar el juego (opcional)

1]   *Añadir más efectos de sonido o cambiar los gráficos y la temática de todo el juego a una de tu preferencia. Ejemplo: Vaqueros*

TETRIX

Inspirado por otro juego estupendo, extremadamente popular y que aún se juega actualmente. Tetris, el sorprendente juego ruso, rompió récords en todo el mundo y venía incluido con la exitosa Game Boy de Nintendo, en mi humilde opinión, el mejor sistema de juego portátil jamás creado. Nuestra versión tendrá un poco más de color. Espero que disfrutes de esta versión simplificada del clásico juego que vino detrás de la Cortina de Hierro. ¡Nostrovia!

Jugadores: 1

Reglas: Haz líneas completas para obtener puntos y limpiar la pantalla.

Controles: z = izquierda, x = derecha, espacio hará rotar algunas de las figuras.

```
  10 REM ******ZX Spectrum Code Club *******
  15 REM * TETRIX by Gary Plowman    2015   *
  20 REM ********************************
  30 INK 0: PAPER 7: BORDER 4
  45 REM ****** Initialising variables
  50 PRINT AT 2,10; INK 7; BRIGHT 1; PAPER 0;"TETRIX": PRINT
AT 4,5;""
  60 PRINT AT 4,5;"Mistakes cost Points!"
  80 PRINT AT 18,5; FLASH 1;"PRESS A KEY TO START": PAUSE 0:
CLS
 100 GO SUB 5000: REM Graphics
 110 GO SUB 300: REM initialise:
 130 GO SUB 1000: REM draw screen
 140 GO SUB 2000: main loop:
 300 LET blocktype=0: LET rotate=0: LET inkcol=0: LET ypos=4:
LET xpos=INT (RND*10)+7: LET rotateproc=3000
```

```
 310 DIM a(3): DIM b(3): DIM c$(3): DIM  d$(3):
 330 LET xpos2=0: LET score=0: LET offset=0: LET mov=0: LET
lines=0
 340 GO SUB 3000
 360 RETURN
1000 REM ****** Screen
1010 FOR n = 6 TO 16: PRINT AT 19,n; PAPER 4; INK 6;CHR$
(146): NEXT n
1020 FOR m =2 TO 19
1030 PRINT AT m,5; PAPER 4; INK 6;CHR$ (146);CHR$ (146);AT
m,16;CHR$ (146);CHR$ (146)
1030 NEXT m
1040 PRINT AT 4,20; PAPER 1; INK 6;"LINES";AT 5,20;lines
1100 RETURN
2000 REM *** MAIN GAME
2005 GO SUB 3600
2008 IF mov=1 THEN GO SUB 3700
2010 LET i$=INKEY$():
2016 LET mov=0
2020 LET atr1=ATTR (ypos,xpos): LET atr2=ATTR (ypos+1,xpos):
LET atr11=ATTR (ypos,xpos+1): LET atr12=ATTR (ypos+1,xpos+1):
LET atr21=ATTR (ypos,xpos+2): LET atr22=ATTR (ypos+1,xpos+2):
2030 IF blocktype<=2 AND (atr1=56 OR atr2=56) AND (atr11=56 OR
atr12=56) AND (atr21=56 OR atr22=56) THEN LET mov=1
2040 IF blocktype>2 AND (atr1=56 OR atr2=56) AND (atr11=56 OR
atr12=56) THEN LET mov=1
2050 IF mov=1 AND i$="z" AND xpos>7 AND ATTR (ypos,xpos-1)=56
THEN GO SUB 3600: LET xpos=xpos-1: LET offset=1
2060 IF mov=1 AND i$="x" AND ((atr11=56 AND ATTR (ypos-
1,xpos+1)=56) OR (atr21=56 AND ATTR (ypos-1,xpos+2)=56) OR
(ATTR (ypos,xpos+3)=56 AND ATTR (ypos-1,xpos+3)=56)) THEN GO
SUB 3600: LET xpos=xpos+1: LET offset=-1
2070 IF i$=" " AND mov=1 THEN GO SUB 4800
2100 LET ypos=ypos+mov
2110 IF mov=0 THEN GO SUB 3500: GO SUB 3000
2205 GO TO 2000
```

```
2210 GO SUB 3000
2600 GO TO 2000
3000 REM rotateoproc
3005 GO SUB 4000: GO SUB 4000: RANDOMIZE
3006 FOR n = 1 TO 3: LET b(n)=0: LET a(n)=0: LET c$(n)="": LET
d$(n)="": NEXT n
3007 IF ypos < 4 THEN BEEP .5,-4: PRINT AT 10,10;"GAME OVER":
PAUSE 0: PAUSE 0: CLS : GO TO 110
3010 LET blocktype=INT (RND*7)
3020 IF blocktype=0 THEN LET b(2)=1: LET a(1)=1: LET a(2)=1:
LET a(3)=1
3030 IF blocktype=1 THEN LET a(1)=1: LET b(1)=1: LET b(2)=1:
LET b(3)=1
3035 IF blocktype=2 THEN LET a(3)=1: LET b(1)=1: LET b(2)=1:
LET b(3)=1
3040 IF blocktype=3 OR blocktype=3 THEN LET b(1)=1: LET
b(2)=1: LET a(1)=1: LET a(2)=1
3050 IF blocktype=4 THEN LET a(1)=1: LET b(1)=1: LET b(2)=1
3070 IF blocktype=5 THEN LET a(2)=1: LET b(1)=1: LET b(2)=1
3075 IF blocktype>5 THEN LET a(1)=1: LET b(1)=1: LET b(2)=1
3080 LET ypos=2: LET xpos=7+INT (RND*3)
3200 RETURN
3500 REM **** PRINT BLOCKS with alternate colour
3505 LET inkbl = INT (blocktype/2)+1
3510 FOR n =1 TO 3
3540 IF a(n)=1 THEN PRINT INK inkbl;AT ypos,xpos+(n-1);CHR$
(145)
3550 IF b(n)=1 THEN PRINT INK inkbl;AT ypos-1,xpos+(n-1);CHR$
(145)
3560 NEXT n
3570 RETURN
3600 REM **** CLEAR BLOCKS
3610 FOR n =1 TO 3
3620 IF a(n)=1 THEN PRINT PAPER 7;AT ypos-1,xpos+(n-
1)+offset;" "
```

```
3630 IF b(n)=1 THEN PRINT PAPER 7;AT ypos-2,xpos+(n-
1)+offset;" "
3660 NEXT n
3665 LET offset=0
3670 RETURN
3700 REM **** PRINT BLOCKS with standard colour
3710 FOR n =1 TO 3
3740 IF a(n)=1 THEN PRINT INK 1; PAPER 7;AT ypos,xpos+(n-
1);CHR$ (145)
3750 IF b(n)=1 THEN PRINT INK 1; PAPER 7;AT ypos-1,xpos+(n-
1);CHR$ (145)
3760 NEXT n
3770 RETURN
4000 REM *** CLEAR LINES
4010 LET count=0
4015 LET count2=0
4020 FOR n=7 TO 15:
4030 IF ATTR (ypos,n)<>56 THEN LET count=count+1
4035 IF ATTR (ypos-1,n)<>56 THEN LET count2=count2+1
4040 NEXT n
4050 IF count=9 THEN LET lines=lines+1
4055 IF count2=9 THEN LET lines=lines+1:
4056 IF count2<9 AND count < 9 THEN RETURN
4057 LET l$=CHR$ (145)+CHR$ (145)+CHR$ (145)+CHR$ (145)+CHR$
(145)+CHR$ (145)+CHR$ (145)+CHR$ (145)+CHR$ (145)
4058 LET score = score + (10*lines*(19-ypos))
4060 FOR n =0 TO 7
4070 BEEP .1,n
4080 IF count=9 THEN PRINT ;AT ypos,7; INK n;l$
4090 IF count2=9 THEN PRINT AT ypos-1,7; INK n;l$
4095 NEXT n:
4101 IF count=9 THEN LET cn=0
4102 IF count2=9 THEN LET  cn=1
4103 PRINT AT ypos-cn,7; INK 0; PAPER 7;"          "
4105 GO SUB 4700
```

```
4110 PRINT AT 5,20; PAPER 1; INK 7;lines;AT 8,20;"SCORE";AT
9,20;score
4120 RETURN
4500 REM *** SHIFT ALL DOWN 1 PLACE
4510 FOR n = ypos TO 4 STEP -1
4520 FOR m= 7 TO 15
4530 IF count2=9 AND ATTR (ypos-n-1,m)>56 THEN PRINT INK 0;
PAPER 7;AT ypos-1-n,m;" ";AT ypos-n+1,m;CHR$ (145)
4540 IF count=9 AND ATTR (ypos-n-1,m)>56 THEN PRINT INK 0;
PAPER 7;AT ypos-n,m;" ";AT ypos-n+1,m;CHR$ (145)
4590 NEXT m
4600 NEXT n
4610 RETURN
4700 REM *** --------------------------SHIFT DOWN
4710 FOR n = ypos-cn TO 3 STEP -1
4720 FOR j = 7 TO 15
4725 LET att=ATTR (n,j)
4730 IF att<>56 THEN PRINT INK att-56; PAPER 7;AT n+1,j;CHR$
(145);AT n,j; INK 0; PAPER 7;" "
4740 NEXT j
4750 NEXT n
4760 RETURN
4800 IF blocktype > 5 THEN LET blocktype=5: BEEP .2,8: GO SUB
3600: LET a(1)=1: LET a(2)=0: GO SUB 3700: RETURN
4810 IF blocktype =5 THEN LET blocktype=6: BEEP .2,8: GO SUB
3600: LET a(2)=1: LET a(1)=0: GO SUB 3700: RETURN
4820 IF blocktype =2 THEN LET blocktype=1: BEEP .2,8: GO SUB
3600: LET a(3)=1: LET a(1)=0: GO SUB 3700: RETURN
4820 IF blocktype =1 THEN LET blocktype=2: BEEP .2,8: GO SUB
3600: LET a(1)=1: LET a(3)=0: GO SUB 3700: RETURN
4840 RETURN
5000 FOR n = 0 TO 23:
5010 READ dat
5020 POKE USR "a"+n,dat
5030 NEXT n
5050 RETURN
```

```
5100 DATA 85,162,85,168,21,170,69,170,255,129,189,165,165
,189,129,255
5110 DATA 255,145,145,145,255,133,133,255
```

¿Qué hay de nuevo?

Empezamos construyendo nuestra pantalla de juego y limitando el movimiento dentro del área de juego. Los elementos bajarán por la pantalla hasta que encuentren el suelo u otro bloque. Luego el siguiente elemento comenzará a bajar una posición a la vez.

Si el área debajo del bloque está ocupada y el bloque no puede encajar, entonces el bloque se quedará allí y controlaremos el siguiente bloque y así sucesivamente.

Todo eso es muy fácil. La parte difícil viene cuando tenemos que coincidir con una línea y derribar el resto de los bloques. Esto se hace con un array, un loop y nuestra amiga, la función ATTR(). SCREEN$() no funcionará con los UDG y no distingue atributos de color como lo hace ATTR().

```
4710 FOR n = ypos-cn TO 3 STEP -1
4720 FOR j = 7 TO 15
4725 LET att=ATTR (n,j)
4730 IF att<>56 THEN PRINT INK att-56; PAPER 7;AT n+1,j;CHR$
(145);AT n,j; INK 0; PAPER 7;" "
4740 NEXT j
4750 NEXT n
```

Arriba se muestra un código simple que se utiliza para cambiar las posiciones y los atributos de color de los bloques anteriores. Nuestro juego Tetrix no es perfecto, pero se pueden añadir más rotaciones en las figuras para mejorarlo. Un enfoque simple lo mantendrá fácil de entender y lo suficientemente corto para escribirlo.

Sugerencias para ampliar el juego (opcional)

1]   Añadir rotaciones a las figuras

2]   Agregar funciones al juego

3]   Añadir más bloques de estilos gráficos o una temática
     diferente al juego

TYPE INVADERS

¿Qué tal un juego que pruebe los reflejos, la ortografía y te ponga bajo presión? Bueno, eso es exactamente lo que hace Type Invaders. Un juego con contenido educativo y que a la vez es una carrera contra el reloj. Compite contra un amigo o miembro de la familia para ver quién obtiene la mejor puntuación mientras tratan de mantener la calma y la compostura.

Jugadores: 1

Reglas: El jugador escribe palabras mientras la base es atacada por el lado derecho de la pantalla.

Controles: Escribe palabras. Cometer un error significa tener que comenzar la palabra nuevamente (pulsando la tecla enter). También es un juego divertido para niños, cuando se usan palabras más pequeñas.

```
  10 REM ******ZX Spectrum Code Club ********
  15 REM * TYPE INVADERS by Gary Plowman     *
  20 REM *********************************
  30 INK 7: PAPER 0: BORDER 4: CLS
  45 REM ****** Initialising variables
  50 PRINT AT 2,10; INK 7; BRIGHT 1; PAPER 0;"TYPE INVADERS":
PRINT AT 4,5;"Type Fast to Keep the Invaders":
  60 PRINT AT 4,5;"Mistakes cost Points!"
  80 PRINT AT 18,5; FLASH 1;"PRESS A KEY TO START": PAUSE 0:
 100 GO SUB 300: REM initialise
 130 GO SUB 1000: REM main loop for game
 200 GO TO 30:
 300 REM ***** SETUP
```

```
 310 LET lives=3: DIM a$(18,20): DIM x(18): DIM y(18): LET
score=0: LET misses=0: LET t$="": LET limit=3: LET lmt=0
 320 RESTORE 340
 305 RANDOMIZE
 330 FOR n=1 TO 18:
 340 READ d$
 350 LET a$(n)=d$: LET y(n)=INT (RND*18)+1
 370 NEXT n
 390 RETURN
1000 CLS : REM ******* MAIN GAME
1010 FOR n = 1 TO 19
1020 PRINT AT n,30; PAPER 6; INK RND*5;CHR$ (139);CHR$ (139)
1030 NEXT n
1031 FOR n = 1 TO 170
1032 PLOT INK RND*6;INT (RND*210),n
1036 NEXT n
1038 PRINT AT 0,0;"        ** TYPE INVADERS **"
1040 LET i$=INKEY$()
1045 LET lmt=0
1050 FOR n = 1 TO 18:
1060 IF x(n)>0 THEN PRINT AT y(n),x(n);" ";a$(n): LET
lmt=lmt+1: LET x(n)=x(n)+.5
1080 IF x(n)=30 THEN GO SUB 2000:
1070 IF i$="" THEN LET i$=INKEY$()
1090 NEXT n
1100 IF lmt<limit THEN LET test=INT (RND*17)+1
1110 IF x(test)=0 THEN LET x(test)=1: LET y(test)=test:
1120 IF i$="" THEN LET i$=INKEY$():
1130 IF i$=CHR$ (13) THEN BEEP .05,4: GO SUB 1500: REM ***
check for match
1200 IF i$<"a" AND i$>"z" THEN GO TO 1040
1205 IF i$<>"" THEN BEEP .02,10
1210 LET t$=t$+i$
1220 PRINT AT 20,0; PAPER 7; INK 2;t$
1230 PRINT AT 20,13; INK 7; BRIGHT 1;"Score:";score;"
Misses:";misses
```

```
1400 GO TO 1040:
1500 REM **** Checking for a hit
1510 LET r$="": LET s$="": LET sc=LEN t$*10
1520 FOR m=1 TO 18
1522 FOR p=1 TO 20-LEN t$
1523 LET t$=t$+" "
1525 NEXT p
1530 IF t$=a$(m) THEN PRINT AT y(m),x(m); PAPER 6; INK
2;"***": LET x(m)=0: LET score=score+sc: LET misses=misses-1:
BEEP .1,14: GO TO 1550
1540 NEXT m
1550 LET t$="": PRINT AT 20,0;"                    ": LET
i$="": LET misses=misses+1
1600 RETURN
2000 REM ***** GAME OVER
2010 PRINT AT 18,13; INK 2;"** BASE DESTROYED **"
2020 PRINT AT 10,10; FLASH 1;"PRESS TO RESTART"
2030 IF INKEY$()="" THEN GO TO 2030
2050 GO TO 100
3000 DATA "fun","fast","type","good","shoot","bang"
3010 DATA "planets","invaders","cosmic","sinclair",
"spectrum","coding"
3020 DATA "missedme","comingtogetu","fireatwill",
"launchmissile","blazingthruster","supercharged"
```

¿Qué hay de nuevo?

Como antes, usamos INKEY$() para capturar las pulsaciones de teclas, pero esta vez
simulamos la entrada de texto y permitimos que la tecla Enter (CHR$(13)) termine la
secuencia de entrada.

```
1120 IF i$="" THEN LET i$=INKEY$():
1130 IF i$=CHR$ (13) THEN BEEP .05,4: GO SUB 1500: REM ***
check for match
```

Otro nuevo comando introducido aquí es LEN. Este devuelve un valor para la longitud de la cadena que se desea consultar.

También utilizamos DATA para almacenar nuestros valores de cadena para nuestras palabras. A continuación se muestra el código utilizado para READ en esas palabras y colocarlas aleatoriamente en la pantalla.

```
330 FOR n=1 TO 18:
 340 READ d$
 350 LET a$(n)=d$: LET y(n)=INT (RND*18)+1
 370 NEXT n
```

Cada cadena del array está asociada con un valor de array, y() para la posición de la pantalla del eje y. Las líneas 1520 a 1540 comprueban la respuesta y llenan la cadena con espacios en blanco que Sinclair BASIC necesita cuando trabaja con arrays de cadenas. Los arrays de cadenas de Sinclair BASIC siempre son fijos en longitud y rellenan cada valor con espacios.

Sugerencias para ampliar el juego (opcional)

1]   Añadir más palabras o cambiar las palabras existentes
2]   Aumentar la velocidad del juego mientras se superan niveles
3]   Distribuir la velocidad de las palabras al azar, para que algunas sean más rápidas que otras y deban ser introducidas primero

MINIPONG

Basado en otro clásico de Arcades y de consolas de casa como el Atari 2600. ¿Quién no recuerda el sonido de la bola cuadrada cuando no golpea la raqueta? Pong, la versión original del arcade, se componía enteramente de chips lógicos discretos (sin CPU) y fue un fenómeno mundial. Esta es una versión corta y sencilla para hacer un clon de pong..

Jugadores: 1

Reglas: Golpea la pelota. ¡Evite fallar para ganar!

Controles: q = arriba, a = abajo

```
  10 REM ******ZX Spectrum Code Club *******
  15 REM * MINIPONG by Gary Plowman         *
  20 REM **************2015*****************
  30 INK 7: PAPER 0: BORDER 0: CLS
  45 REM ****** Initialising variables
  50 PRINT AT 2,10; INK 7; BRIGHT 1; PAPER 2;"MINI PONG":
PAUSE 0
  35 LET lives=3
 100 GO SUB 300: REM initialise
 120 GO SUB 500: REM menu
 130 GO SUB 1000: REM main loop for game
 200 GO TO 30
 300 LET ply=2: LET win=0: DIM a(9,2): DIM d(30): LET lvl=1:
LET posy=30: LET y=10: LET y2=10: LET frm=0: LET score=0: LET
score2=0: LET time=0: LET mov=11: LET ball=0: LET vx=0: LET
vy=0: LET p$=CHR$ (143)
```

```
 400 RETURN
 500 CLS
 510 LET w$=CHR$ (140)
 520 FOR n = 0 TO 31
 530 PRINT INK 7;AT 1,n;w$;AT 21,n;w$
 540 NEXT n
 542 LET w$=CHR$ (136)
 545 FOR n = 2 TO 20 STEP 2
 546 PRINT INK 7; AT n,15;w$
 549 NEXT n
 550 RETURN
1000 IF score=10 OR score2=10 THEN PRINT AT 10,10; FLASH 1;"G
A M E   O V E R";AT 12,10;"RESTARTING": PAUSE 0: GO TO 30: REM
Main Loop
1002 LET bx=10: LET by=10
1003 PRINT AT 0,10;score;AT 0,18;score2
1005 PRINT AT y-1,2;" ";AT y,2;p$;AT y+1,2;p$;AT y+2,2;" "
1008 PRINT AT y2-1,27;" ";AT y2,27;p$;AT y2+1,27;p$;AT
y2+2,27;" "
1010 LET i$=INKEY$(): LET kemp=IN 31
1120 IF (i$="q" OR kemp=8) AND y>3 THEN LET y=y-1
1130 IF (i$="a" OR kemp=4) AND y<18 THEN LET y=y+1
1150 GO SUB 2000: REM ************Move Ball
1180 GO SUB 2500: REM ************Player 2 AI
1400 GO TO 1005
2000 REM *** Move Ball
2010 IF vx=0 AND vy=0 THEN LET vx=-1: LET vy=(RND*2)-(RND*2):
BEEP .1,4
2030 PRINT AT by,bx;" "
2038 LET collide = ABS (by-y): LET collide2 = ABS (by-y2)
2040 IF by+vy>19 THEN LET vy=-1*(vy)
2050 IF by+vy<3 THEN LET vy=-1*(vy)
2055 IF bx+vx>27 AND collide2>1 THEN LET score=score+1: LET
vx=0: LET vy=0: BEEP 1,0: GO TO 1000
2060 IF bx+vx<3 AND ABS collide>1 THEN LET score2=score2+1:
BEEP 1,0: GO TO 1000
```

```
2065 IF bx+vx>27 AND collide2<1 THEN LET vx=-1*(vx): LET
vy=(RND*3)-(RND*3): BEEP .2,4
2070 IF bx+vx<3 AND collide<1 THEN LET vx=-1*(vx): LET
vy=(RND*3)-(RND*3): BEEP .2,4
2080 LET bx=bx+vx: LET by=by+vy:
2090 PRINT AT by,bx;p$
2100 RETURN
2500 REM **** PLAYER 2 movement
2510 IF y2>by+vy AND bx>9 THEN LET y2=y2-.8
2520 IF y2<by+vy AND bx>9 THEN LET y2=y2+.8
2550 RETURN
```

¿Qué hay de Nuevo?

Movimientos básicos de la IA ante su oponente. El rebote se logra al usar una inversión del valor de la dirección horizontal o vertical. Para aumentar la dificultad, puede incrementar la velocidad del jugador 2.

```
2500 REM **** PLAYER 2 movement
2510 IF y2>by+vy AND bx>9 THEN LET y2=y2-.8
2520 IF y2<by+vy AND bx>9 THEN LET y2=y2+.8
```

Sugerencias para ampliar el juego (opcional)

1]   Incrementar la dificultad
2]   Añadir obstáculos para variar el rebote
3]   Modificar para que un jugador controle los dos jugadores con un solo mando
4]   Agregar más opciones de color

TAKEAWAY TED

Ted debe administrar su tienda muy bien o corre el riesgo de perder clientes y dinero. Su chica también le dará su merecido si se termina arruinando. Ted debe alimentar a los clientes con las órdenes adecuadas. Si se hace una cola de comida, entonces Ted ahorrará dinero en los costes de operación. Si le da al cliente la comida equivocada... ¡Oh, oh!

Jugadores: 1

Reglas: Comienza tu cola y mientras los clientes entran en la tienda, habrá que hacer coincidir sus órdenes con el orden que le corresponde..

Letras en la pantalla: C = Patatas, B = Hamburguesa, F = Pescado, P = Pizza y K = Kebab

Haz que los pedidos coincidan con la cola de clientes. La tecla 'K' generará una nueva lista de alimentos, pero costará dinero. El uso de todos los artículos disponibles proporciona una lista gratuita de alimentos para servir. Si das una orden incorrecta a un cliente, perderás dinero. Mantener la tienda abierta cuesta dinero, así que hay que hacerlo bien.

Controles: K = hacer hasta 5 alimentos. Selección de alimentos: teclas a, b, c, d o e para seleccionar alimentos. Teclas 1 - 8 para entregar el artículo a los clientes.

```
10 REM ******ZX Spectrum Code Club ******
15 REM * TAKEAWAY TED (Chip Shop Sim)    *
20 REM ******** Gary Plowman 2015 ********
30 INK 2: PAPER 0: BORDER 0: CLS
45 REM ****** Initialising variables
```

```
  50 PRINT AT 1,8;"TAKEAWAY TED": PAUSE 0
  35 DIM p(2): DIM l(10): DIM c(8): LET cash=30: LET
speed=100: DIM c$(8): LET cust=0: DIM q$(5): LET k$="CBFPK":
LET take = 0: LET timer=20: LET score=0
 100 GO SUB 300: REM initialise and start game
 130 GO SUB 1000: REM main loop for game
 200 GO TO 30
 300 REM *** DRAW SCREEN
 310 CLS
 320 INK 6: PLOT 20,150: DRAW 0,-100: DRAW 200,0: DRAW 0,100:
PLOT 30,70: DRAW 180,0: DRAW 0,80: PLOT 30,70: DRAW 0,80
 325 INK 4: PLOT 100,104: DRAW 0,15: DRAW 15,0: DRAW 0,-15:
DRAW -15,0: PLOT 105,114: DRAW 0,-5: PLOT 110,114: DRAW 0,-5
 326 INK 6: PLOT 107,102: DRAW 0,-7: DRAW -5,0
 327 PLOT 112,102: DRAW 0,-9: DRAW -5,0:
 330 PRINT AT 20,12; PAPER 2; INK 7;"Door":
 340 INK 3: PRINT AT 20,0; PAPER 6;"Ted's Chips";AT 20,17;"
Take Away "
 350 PRINT AT 14,19;" Counter"
 360 PRINT AT 14,3;"12345678":
 370 INK 4: PRINT AT 0,10;"CASH: $";cash; "   Sc:"; score
 380 FOR n = 1 TO 5: PRINT AT 2+n,4; INK 6;CHR$ (64+n): NEXT n
 390 REM ** draw more...
 400 INK 5: PLOT 120,130: DRAW -34,0:
 410 PLOT 140,130: DRAW 0,30: FOR n = 10 TO 30 STEP 4: PLOT
137,130+n: DRAW 7,0: NEXT n
 420 PRINT AT 4,11;"Oven";AT 2,19;"Kebab";AT 2,0; BRIGHT
1;"K=New Food"
 430 PRINT INK 6;AT 6,18;"_menu__"; BRIGHT 1;AT 7,17;"Chips
$2";AT 8,17;"Burger $3";AT 9,17;"Fish   $5";AT 10,17;"Pizza
$8";AT 11,17;"Kebab  $4"
 500 RETURN
1000 LET a$=INKEY$(): LET timer=timer-1
1002 IF timer<0 AND INT (RND*4)>2 THEN LET c$(INT (RND*8)+1)="
"
1005 IF timer<0 THEN LET timer=10: LET cash=cash-1
```

```
1008 IF a$="" THEN GO TO 3800
1110 IF a$="k" THEN GO SUB 4200: GO SUB 4100
1120 IF a$="a" THEN LET take=1: PRINT AT 3,7;"-": BEEP .3,5
1130 IF a$="b" THEN LET take=2: PRINT AT 4,7;"-": BEEP .3,5
1140 IF a$="c" THEN LET take=3: PRINT AT 5,7;"-": BEEP .3,5
1150 IF a$="d" THEN LET take=4: PRINT AT 6,7;"-": BEEP .3,5
1160 IF a$="e" THEN LET take=5: PRINT AT 7,7;"-": BEEP .3,5:
1170 IF take>0 AND a$>="1" AND a$<="8" THEN GO SUB 4700: GO
SUB 4100
3800 GO SUB 4300
3810 GO SUB 4600
3900 GO TO 1000
4100 REM *** PRINT KITCHEN QUEUE
4110 INK 2: FOR n = 1 TO 5
4120 PRINT AT 2+n,6;q$(n);" "
4130 NEXT n
4150 RETURN
4200 REM *** ADD TO QUEUE
4205 LET cash = cash - 5
4206 RANDOMIZE
4208 FOR n = 1 TO 8
4210 LET r =INT (RND*10): LET qpos =INT (RND*5)+1
4220 IF r = 1 OR r=6 THEN LET q$(qpos)="B"
4230 IF r = 2 OR r=7 THEN LET q$(qpos)="C"
4240 IF r = 3 THEN LET q$(qpos)="F"
4250 IF r = 4 THEN LET q$(qpos)="K"
4252 IF r = 5 THEN LET q$(qpos)="P"
4255 BEEP .02,qpos
4260 NEXT n
4290 RETURN
4300 REM **** RECALC SCREEN
4310 INK 4: PRINT AT 0,10;"CASH: $";cash;"  ";" Sc:";score
4320 FOR n = 1 TO 8
4330 PRINT BRIGHT 1;AT 16,2+n;c$(n)
4340 NEXT n
```

```
4400 RETURN
4600 REM **** NEW CUSTOMER?
4610 RANDOMIZE : LET r =INT (RND*20)
4620 LET p =INT (RND*8)+1
4630 LET order=INT (RND*5)+1
4640 IF r>4 THEN RETURN
4650 IF c$(p)=" " THEN LET c$(p)=k$(order)
4690 RETURN
4700 REM **** GIVE OUT ORDER
4705 BEEP .2,11
4710 LET qpos =VAL a$
4720 IF q$(take)="C" THEN LET price=2
4730 IF q$(take)="B" THEN LET price=3
4740 IF q$(take)="P" THEN LET price=8
4750 IF q$(take)="F" THEN LET price=5
4760 IF q$(take)="K" THEN LET price=4
4765 IF c$(qpos)<>q$(take) THEN GO TO 4820
4770 IF c$(qpos)=q$(take) AND q$(take)<>" " THEN LET cash =
cash + price: LET c$(qpos)=" ": LET q$(take)="-": LET take=0:
LET score=score+1
4775 LET count=0
4780 FOR n = 1 TO 5
4785 IF q$(n)=" " OR q$(n)="-" THEN LET count=count+1
4790 NEXT n
4800 IF count=5 THEN LET cash=cash+5: GO SUB 4200
4810 RETURN
4820 LET cash = cash - 10: LET c$(qpos)=" ": LET q$(take)="-":
LET take=0
4900 RETURN
```

¿Qué hay de nuevo?

¿Quién no ama una bolsa de patatas fritas? Este es un juego basado en cola que necesita reflejos rápidos para atender a los clientes. Este juego puede causar dolor de cabeza.

Hemos creado gráficos con PLOTs y DRAWs en lugar de UDG, ya que no hay ninguna pantalla de acción por la que preocuparse.

```
326 INK 6: PLOT 107,102: DRAW 0,-7: DRAW -5,0
```

DRAW tiene un tercer parámetro que se utiliza para proporcionar el ángulo de la línea. No lo usamos, pero es práctico saber que está allí en caso de que planee probar algo con él.

Sugerencias para ampliar el juego (opcional)

1] *Incrementar dificultad*

2] *Agregar más elementos o cambiar la temática*

3] *Aumentar la locura hasta 11*

C5 SOLAR RACE

Sir Clive Sinclair financió con éxito su Kickstarter para construir 4 C5s solares y usarlas en su carrera anual Sinclair C5 Solar. Los cuatro competidores corren más de 200 metros para ganar el codiciado trofeo que es entregado por el propio Sir Clive. El trofeo se construye enteramente de cubiertas plásticas blancas pre-usadas del ZX80.

Jugadores: 2

Reglas: Hasta cuatro jugadores. Presiona el número de tu coche para aumentar la velocidad. Si te quedas sin energía debes permitir que el sol regenere la batería.

Controles: Teclas 1 a 4.

```
  10 REM ******************
  20 REM *  C5 Solar Race *
  30 REM *  Gary Plowman   *
  40 REM ******************
 100 PAPER 7: INK 0: BORDER 7: BRIGHT 1: CLS :
 140 GO SUB 300: REM setup game
 150 GO SUB 1000: REM draw screen
 160 GO SUB 2000: REM main loop:
 300 LET a$=CHR$  136: LET b$=CHR$ 139+CHR$ 142+CHR$ 140+CHR$
134: LET c$=CHR$ 142+CHR$  140+CHR$  140+CHR$ 140+CHR$ 138:
 310 LET s$=CHR$  143+CHR$ 143: LET t$=CHR$  143+CHR$ 143+CHR$
143+CHR$ 143: DIM p(4): DIM x(4): LET dist=0
 320 FOR n =1 TO 4: LET p(n)=10: LET x(n)=1: NEXT n
```

```
 330 LET ply=1: LET l$="": LET q$="": LET redraw=0
 340 FOR n=1 TO 31: LET l$=l$+CHR$  132: LET q$=q$+CHR$ 136:
NEXT n:
1000 PRINT INK 6;AT 0,24;s$;AT 1,23;t$;AT 2,23;t$;AT
3,23;t$;AT 4,24;s$
1010 FOR n = 5 TO 17: PRINT AT n,0; INK 7; PAPER 0;"
": NEXT n
1020 FOR n = 1 TO 4
1050 PRINT PAPER 0; INK 7;AT n*3+2,x(n);a$;AT n*3+3,x(n);b$;AT
n*3+4,x(n);c$;AT n*3+2,x(n); INK n+1;CHR$ 143
1060 NEXT n
1080 PRINT AT 0,0;"Players 1 - 4 for Boost";AT 4,0;"200m
Race!"
1090 RANDOMIZE
1100 LET i$=INKEY$():
1105 PRINT AT 1,0;dist;"m": LET dist=dist+1
1110 GO SUB 2000: REM anim screen
1115 GO SUB 2500: REM accelerate
1118 IF dist>200 THEN GO SUB 5000
1120 IF i$<"1" OR i$>"4" THEN GO TO 1100
1130 LET v=VAL i$
1140 IF p(v)>2 THEN LET p(v)=p(v)-INT (RND*3): LET
x(v)=x(v)+.5: BEEP .01,5
1150 IF p(v)<2 THEN LET x(v)=x(v)-2: LET p(v)=2: BEEP .01,-5:
1180 GO SUB 3500
1190 GO SUB 3000
1900 GO TO 1100
2000 REM *** Screen anim
2010 IF ATTR (18,0)<69 THEN  PRINT AT 18,0; INK 5; PAPER 0;l$:
RETURN
2010 PRINT AT 18,0; INK 0; PAPER 0;" "; INK 5;q$
2020 FOR n = 1 TO 4
2030 IF p(n)<9 THEN LET p(n)=p(n)+.4
2040 NEXT n
2100 RETURN
2500 REM *** Acc
```

```
2510 LET choose=INT (RND*4)+1
2520 LET x(choose)=x(choose)+RND*2
2530 LET v=choose: GO SUB 3500
2570 RETURN
3000 REM *** power bar
3005 PRINT AT 20,0; INK 2;"P";v
3010 FOR n = 1 TO p(v): PRINT AT 20,n+3; INK 2;CHR$ 138;"
": NEXT n
3020 RETURN
3500 REM *** ReDraw C5 Buggy
3510 IF x(1)>25 OR x(2)>25 OR x(3)>25 OR x(4)>25 THEN GO SUB
3800: GO SUB 3700: REM ** Scroll Screen
3550 LET pos=v*3+2:
3560 PRINT PAPER 0; INK 7;AT pos,x(v)-2;"   ";AT pos+1,x(v)-2;"
";AT pos+2,x(v)-2;"   "
3570 PRINT PAPER 0; INK 7;AT v*3+2,x(v);a$;AT v*3+3,x(v);b$;AT
v*3+4,x(v);c$;AT v*3+2,x(v); INK v+1;CHR$ 143:
3600 RETURN
3700 REM *** Scroll
3710 FOR n =1 TO 4: LET x(n)=x(n)-10
3720 IF x(n)<0 THEN LET x(n)=2
3730 NEXT n
3760 RETURN
3800 REM *** redraw
3810 FOR n =1 TO 4
3820 PRINT PAPER 0; INK 7;AT n*3+2,x(n)-2;"         ";AT
n*3+3,x(n)-2;"         ";AT n*3+4,x(n)-2;"         "
3830 IF x(n)<2 THEN LET x(n)=2
3840 NEXT n
3850 RETURN
5000 REM *** Declare winner
5010 LET win=0: LET winner=0
5020 FOR n =1 TO 4
5030 IF x(n)> win THEN LET win=x(n): LET winner=n
5040 NEXT n
5050 PRINT AT 10,10;"WINNER IS"
```

```
5060 PRINT AT 12,10;"Player ";winner: BEEP 2,8: PAUSE 0: GO TO
100
5070 RETURN
```

Hacer el prototipo de un juego

El uso de gráficos básicos para un juego es una buena manera de probar la idea antes de invertir demasiado tiempo en hacer un montón de programación. BASIC es muy divertido para la creación de prototipos. Un prototipo es como un modelo crudo de demostración. La próxima vez que pienses en alguna idea para un juego, trata de hacerla en BASIC y así sabrás si es divertido. Si lo es, entonces probablemente tengas una buena excusa para convertir tu idea en un juego.

Gráficos sencillos de Bloques

Los gráficos de bloque se consideran retro y el aspecto de Minecraft es muy popular actualmente. Puedes utilizar los caracteres de gráficos de Spectrum para crear gráficos sencillos en tus juegos, lo que te ahorrará la necesidad de crear UDG innecesarios para formas sencillas.

__Sugerencias para ampliar el juego (opcional)__

1]   Más C5's
2]   Usar la imaginación y volverse loco

PENALTY SHOOTOUT

> *Todo el mundo ama una buena tanda de penaltis. Aquí podrás programar tu propia versión para 2 jugadores. La sincronización lo es todo en este pequeño pero divertido juego. Espero que no te pelees con tus amigos mientras lo juegan. Pasa un buen rato y no caigas en frustración.*

Jugadores: 2

Reglas: Jugador 1 en azul, jugador 2 en rojo. Los jugadores van por turnos y el ganador será el primero con 5 anotaciones, siempre y cuando su oponente esté 2 por detrás de él. Mientras un jugador dispara, el otro tiene la misión de detener los disparos.

Controles: S = Disparar (trate de no fallar), G = Detener.

```
  10 REM ******ZX Spectrum Code Club *******
  15 REM * PENALTY SHOOTOUT - G Plowman     *
  20 REM *********************************
  30 INK 1: PAPER 4: BORDER 4: CLS
  45 REM ****** Initialising variables
  50 PRINT AT 1,5; INK 7; BRIGHT 1; PAPER 2;"PENALTY
SHOOTOUT": PAUSE 0
  35 LET lives=3: LET dice=0: LET ply=1: DIM p(2): DIM l(10):
DIM c(2): LET miss=0
 100 GO SUB 300: REM initialise
 120 GO SUB 500: REM menu
 130 GO SUB 1000: REM main loop for game
 200 GO TO 30
 300 PRINT AT 2,8; INK 1; BRIGHT 1;"0123456789";AT 10,8; INK
1; BRIGHT 1;"0123456789":
```

```
 320 FOR n = 1 TO 3: PRINT AT 3+n,0; INK n;"OoOoOooOo";AT
3+n,10; PAPER 7;"         "; PAPER 4; INK n+1;" OoOoOooOo": NEXT
n
 330 PRINT AT 6,0; PAPER 2;"==========";AT 6,16;"=========="
 340 PLOT 80,190-(6*8): DRAW 10,-14: PLOT 80+6*8,190-(6*8):
DRAW -10,-14
1000 PRINT AT 18,10;"               ": FOR n = 1 TO INT
(RND*15)+4: BEEP .1,n: NEXT n
1001 IF ply=1 THEN PRINT AT 16,0;"PLAYER 1 to (s)hoot (score
is ";p(1);")"
1002 IF ply=2 THEN PRINT AT 16,0;"PLAYER 2 to (s)hoot (score
is ";p(2);")"
1003 PRINT AT 20,0; PAPER 7;"Ply 1:";p(1);"   Ply 2:";p(2):
1005 BEEP .3,10: LET inkc = 1: IF ply=2 THEN LET inkc=2:
1006 PRINT INK inkc; AT 10,6;CHR$ (139);AT 11,5;CHR$
(137);CHR$ (143);CHR$ (134);AT 12,6;CHR$ (142)
1010 FOR n = 1 TO 10
1020 LET i$=INKEY$()
1030 PRINT AT 11,8+(n-2); INK 6;" ";CHR$ (143);" "
1040 IF i$="s" THEN GO TO 1100
1045 NEXT n: PRINT AT 11,16;"   "
1050 GO TO 1010
1090 BEEP .3,10
1100 IF ply=1 THEN PRINT AT 16,0; INK 2;"PLAYER 2 to save
(g)oal            "
1102 IF ply=2 THEN PRINT AT 16,0; INK 1;"PLAYER 1 to save
(g)aol            "
1110 FOR m = 1 TO 10
1120 LET i$=INKEY$()
1130 PRINT AT 3,8+(m-2); INK 6;" ";CHR$ (143);" "
1140 IF i$="g" THEN GO TO 1200
1145 NEXT m: PRINT AT 3,16;"   "
1150 GO TO 1110
1200 LET c(ply) = c(ply) + 1 : LET miss=0
1210 IF n=m THEN PRINT AT 18,10;"S A V E D!": LET miss=1:
```

```
1220 IF n<>m OR (n<3 OR n>7) THEN PRINT AT 18,10;"Wide!!
": LET miss=1
1225 IF n<>m AND (n>2 AND n<8) THEN PRINT AT 18,10; INK 2;"G O
A L !!! ": LET miss=0
1230 REM IF ply =1 AND miss=1
1240 IF ply =1 AND miss=0 THEN LET p(ply)=p(ply)+1: BEEP 1,14
1250 REM IF ply =2 AND miss=1 THEN LET l(c(ply))=0
1260 IF ply =2 AND miss=0 THEN LET p(ply)=p(ply)+1: BEEP 1,14
1270 IF miss=1 THEN BEEP 1,-1
1275 IF miss=9 THEN BEEP 1,-1
1276 PRINT AT 11,9;"              ";AT 3,9;"           "
1280 IF ply=1 THEN LET ply=2: GO SUB 2000
1290 IF ply=2 THEN LET ply=1: GO SUB 2000
1300 GO TO 1000:
2000 REM ** CHECK FOR WINNER
2010 IF p(1)<5 AND p(2)<5 THEN GO TO 1000
2020 IF p(1)>=5 AND p(1)-p(2)>=2 THEN LET win=1: GO SUB 3000
2030 IF p(2)>=5 AND p(2)-p(1)>=2 THEN LET win=2: GO SUB 3000
2050 RETURN
3000 REM *** WINNER
3010 PRINT AT 10,10; FLASH 1;"WINNER IS PLAYER ";win:
3020 PAUSE 0: PAUSE 0: CLS
3030 BEEP 2,10
3050 GO TO 45
```

Sugerencias para ampliar el juego (opcional)

1] *Añadir mejores gráficos*
2] *Cambiar el juego por completo y hacer un juego de fútbol, con la parte del penalti como la escena para anotar el gol*

BILLY BOB'S GOLD

Este pequeño juego es una mezcla de varios juegos. Parte Hungry Horace, parte Pacman, parte carrera contra el reloj. Tu mina está bajo la amenaza de tres bandidos. Te buscan para sacarte de la mina y así poder quedarse con todo el oro.

Jugadores: 1

Reglas: Recoge el oro de la mina de Billy Bob mientras evitas a los bandidos. Ten cuidado con el tiempo.

Controles: q = arriba, a = abajo, o = izquierda, p = derecha. También se puede usar el mando si está conectado como Kempston.

```
  10 REM ********** ZX Code Club **********
  20 REM * Billy Bob's Gold - Gary Plowman *
  25 REM *********************************
  30 INK 6: PAPER 0: BORDER 0: BRIGHT 1: CLS
  40 GO SUB 6000
  50 PRINT AT 2,6; INK 7; BRIGHT 1; PAPER 0;"BILLY BOB'S
GOLD": PRINT AT 4,5;""
  60 PRINT AT 6,0;"Collect gold beware the outlaws";AT
8,0;"Gold nuggets slow the Timer!"
  80 PRINT AT 18,5; FLASH 1;"PRESS A KEY TO START": PAUSE 0:
CLS : RANDOMIZE : INK 0
 110 GO SUB 300: REM initialise:
 130 GO SUB 1000: REM draw screen
 140 GO SUB 2000: REM main loop
 300 REM *******
 305 LET score=0: LET maxgold=0
 310 LET x= 7: LET y=17: LET vy=0: LET vx=0: LET timer=99
```

```
 320 LET ex1=2: LET ex2 = 22: LET e$=".": LET f$=".": LET
ey1=4: LET ey2=4
 330 LET vx1=0: LET vx2=0: LET vy1=0: LET vy2=0: LET vx3=0:
LET vy3=0: LET ey3=18: LET ex3=22: LET h$="."
 340 LET r3=0
 400 RETURN
1000 REM ****** Screen
1010 CLS : INK 7: PAPER 0: PRINT INK 4;AT 0,0;"     Billy
Bob's Gold"
1015 INK 0
1020 PRINT AT 03,0;"MMMMMMMMMMMMMMMMMMMMMMMMMM"
1030 PRINT AT 04,0;"M                        M"
1040 PRINT AT 05,0;"M MMMMMMM  M  MMMMMM   M"
1050 PRINT AT 06,0;"M            M M M       M"
1060 PRINT AT 07,0;"M M MMMM M  M  M MM MM   M"
1070 PRINT AT 08,0;"M M                 MM  M"
1080 PRINT AT 09,0;"M MMMMMMM  M  MMMM MM   M"
1090 PRINT AT 10,0;"M           M      M      M"
1100 PRINT AT 11,0;"MMMM     M   MMM      MMMM"
1110 PRINT AT 12,0;"M                    M  M"
1115 PRINT AT 13,0;"M MMMM MMM  M  MMMMMM   M"
1120 PRINT AT 14,0;"M                       M"
1125 PRINT AT 15,0;"MM MMMMMMM   M  MMMMMM MM"
1130 PRINT AT 16,0;"M             M          M"
1140 PRINT AT 17,0;"M MMMMMMM  M  MMM MMM   M"
1145 PRINT AT 18,0;"M                       M"
1150 PRINT AT 19,0;"MMMMMMMMMMMMMMMMMMMMMMMMMM"
1155 INK 7
1160 FOR n=3 TO 19
1170 FOR m = 0 TO 25
1180 IF SCREEN$ (n,m)="M" THEN PRINT AT n,m; PAPER 1; INK
1;"M"
1185 IF SCREEN$ (n,m)=" " THEN PRINT AT n,m; INK 6;"."
1190 NEXT m: NEXT n
2000 REM GAME LOOP *********************************************
2010 LET i$=INKEY$: LET j=IN 31
```

```
2110 IF (i$="q" OR j=8) THEN LET vy=-1: LET vx=0
2120 IF (i$="a" OR j=4) THEN LET vy=1: LET vx=0
2130 IF (i$="o" OR j=1) THEN LET vx=-1: LET vy=0
2140 IF (i$="p" OR j=2) THEN LET vx=1: LET vy=0
2190 IF SCREEN$ (y+vy,x+vx)<>"M" THEN PRINT AT y,x;" ": LET
x=x+vx: LET y=y+vy
2195 LET y$=SCREEN$ (y,x)
2200 IF y$="." THEN LET score= score +1: LET timer=timer+1:
LET maxgold=maxgold+1: BEEP .01,8
2240 IF timer> 160 THEN LET timer=160:
2290 PRINT AT y,x;CHR$ (144);AT 20,18;"Clock:";timer;" ";AT
2,0; INK 6;"Score:";score
2300 LET timer=timer-1
2310 IF timer <= 0 THEN PRINT AT 10,10;"GAME OVER";AT
12,10;"SCORE WAS ";score: BEEP 2,10: CLS : GO TO 50
2400 IF maxgold=score THEN LET maxgold=maxgold*2: PRINT AT
10,10;"NEXT LEVEL": BEEP 1,8: BEEP .5,10: GO SUB 310: GO TO
130
2420 PRINT AT ey1,ex1; INK 6;CHR$ (145);AT ey2,ex2; INK 5;CHR$
(145);AT ey3,ex3; INK 4;CHR$ (145)
2430 GO SUB 4000:
3000 GO TO 2000
3010 REM
*************************************************************
4000 REM **** MOVE ENEMIES
4010 LET r1=0: LET r2=0: LET r3=0: RANDOMIZE
4020 IF (vx1=0 AND vy1=0) OR (ex1=11 OR ex1=14) THEN LET
r1=INT (RND*4)+1
4025 IF (vx2=0 AND vy2=0) OR (ex2=11 OR ex2=14) THEN LET
r2=INT (RND*4)+1
4030 IF (vx3=0 AND vy3=0) OR (ex3=11 OR ex3=14) THEN LET
r3=INT (RND*4)+1:
4040 REM IF ABS (vy-vy1)<4 AND ABS (vy-vy1)<4 THEN LET vx1=vx
AND vy1=vy
4060 IF vy1=0 AND r1=1 THEN LET vx1 =-1: GO TO 4080
4065 IF vy1=0 AND r1=2 THEN LET vx1 =1: GO TO 4080
```

```
4070 IF vy1=0 AND r1=3 THEN LET vy1 =-1: GO TO 4080
4075 IF vy1=0 AND r1=4 THEN LET vy1 =1
4080 IF vy2=0 AND r2=1 THEN LET vx2 =-1: GO TO 4120
4095 IF vy2=0 AND r2=2 THEN LET vx2 =1: GO TO 4120
4100 IF vy2=0 AND r2=3 THEN LET vy2 =-1: GO TO 4120
4110 IF vy2=0 AND r2=4 THEN LET vy2 =1
4120 IF vy3=0 AND r3=1 THEN LET vx3 =-1: GO TO 4200
4135 IF vy3=0 AND r3=2 THEN LET vx3 =1: GO TO 4200
4140 IF vy3=0 AND r3=3 THEN LET vy3 =-1: GO TO 4200
4150 IF vy3=0 AND r3=4 THEN LET vy3 =1
4200 REM *** move ::
4210 PRINT INK 6; AT ey1,ex1;e$;AT ey2,ex2;f$;AT ey3,ex3;h$:
4215 IF SCREEN$ (ey1+vy1,ex1+vx1)="M" THEN LET vy1=0: LET
vx1=0
4216 IF SCREEN$ (ey2+vy2,ex2+vx2)="M" THEN LET vy2=0: LET
vx2=0
4218 IF SCREEN$ (ey3+vy3,ex3+vx3)="M" THEN LET vy3=0: LET
vx3=0:
4220 LET ex1 = ex1 + vx1: LET ey1=ey1+vy1
4230 LET ex2 = ex2 + vx2: LET ey2=ey2+vy2
4232 LET ex3 = ex3 + vx3: LET ey3=ey3+vy3
4235 LET e$=SCREEN$ (ey1,ex1): LET f$=SCREEN$ (ey2,ex2): LET
h$=SCREEN$ (ey3,ex3)
4240 PRINT AT ey1,ex1; INK 6;CHR$ (145);AT ey2,ex2; INK 5;CHR$
(145);AT ey3,ex3; INK 4;CHR$ (145)
4250 IF ABS (x-ex1)<2 AND ABS (y-ey1)<2 THEN GO SUB 4600
4260 IF ABS (x-ex2)<2 AND ABS (y-ey2)<2 THEN GO SUB 4600
4270 IF ABS (x-ex3)<2 AND ABS (y-ey3)<2 THEN GO SUB 4600
4410 RETURN
4600 REM ***** GAME OVER
4610 PRINT AT 10,10;"GAME OVER";AT 12,10;"SCORE WAS ";score
4620 FOR n = 1 TO 10: BEEP n/10,n: NEXT n
4630 CLS
4640 GO TO 50
4650 RETURN
5999 REM **** GRAPHICS
```

```
6000 FOR n = 0 TO 15
6010 READ dat
6020 POKE USR "a"+n,dat
6030 NEXT n
6040 RETURN
6100 DATA  24,60,24,27,15,11,24,60,24,126,36,153,126, 24,36,36
```

¿Qué hay de nuevo?

Observa que hemos utilizado ABS una vez más para probar la colisión, en este caso con los bandidos.

```
4250 IF ABS (x-ex1)<2 AND ABS (y-ey1)<2 THEN GO SUB 4600
```

Hemos añadido IA muy básico para cambiar la dirección del bandido al azar, con el fin de mezclar el movimiento de los bandidos.

```
4020 IF (vx1=0 AND vy1=0) OR (ex1=11 OR ex1=14) THEN LET
r1=INT (RND*4)+1
```

Juegos de laberintos

¿Quién no ama los juegos de laberintos? En la década de 1980 todos se volvieron locos por un icono que comía puntos. Así que hemos añadido tres malos con IA básica y rudimentaria (al azar) y unas cuantas modificaciones para hacer que los bandidos pasen por la parte central del laberinto en la pantalla. Mucho se puede hacer con este, nuestro último juego de este libro.

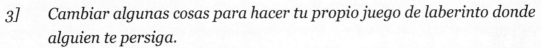

Sugerencias para ampliar el juego (opcional)

1] *Incrementar dificultad*

2] *Añadir otro bandido*

3] *Cambiar algunas cosas para hacer tu propio juego de laberinto donde alguien te persiga.*

Enhorabuena

¡Te has convertido en un *Programador Sinclair BASIC certificado!*

Gracias por comprar este libro y por tomarte el tiempo para trabajar con él. Si ya has pasado por todos los juegos, entonces debes estar muy familiarizado con BASIC y serás capaz de escribir programas por ti mismo. Planifica tus juegos en papel y luego escribe tu código pieza por pieza.

Espero que te hayas divertido y aprendido a lo largo del camino, mientras escribías estos juegos. Espero que hayas disfrutado la experiencia y hayas conseguido que tus neuronas trabajen para crear tus propios juegos con Sinclair BASIC. O quizás te sirva de inspiración para embarcarte en otros lenguajes de codificación.

No te olvides de revisar nuestros juegos para Android. Sólo busca Gazzapper Games en la Playstore. También te agradecemos si dejas una reseña de este libro en la tienda donde lo hayas comprado.

Puedes seguirnos en www.Twitter.com/Gazzapper o visitar nuestro sitio www.gazzapper.com y registrarte para obtener actualizaciones.

Muchas gracias,

Gary Plowman

ANEXO A – El mapa de caracteres

Este es el mapa de caracteres de Spectrum completo, con códigos en decimal.

Ejemplo: PRINT CHR(38) mostrará el carácter &

Código	Carácter				
0	No utilizado	18	FLASH control	36	$
1	No utilizado	19	BRIGHT control	37	%
2	No utilizado	20	INVERSE control	38	&
3	No utilizado	21	OVER control	39	'
4	No utilizado	22	AT control	40	(
5	No utilizado	23	TAB control	41	)
6	PRINT coma	24	No utilizado	42	*
7	EDIT	25	No utilizado	43	+
8	←	26	No utilizado	44	,
9	→	27	No utilizado	45	-
10	↓	28	No utilizado	46	.
11	↑	29	No utilizado	47	/
12	DELETE	30	No utilizado	48	0
13	ENTER	31	No utilizado	49	1
14	número	32	espacio	50	2
15	No utilizado	33	!	51	3
16	INK control	34	"	52	4
17	PAPER control	35	#	53	5
				54	6

55	7		78	N		101	E
56	8		79	O		102	F
57	9		80	P		103	g
58	:		81	Q		104	h
59	;		82	R		105	i
60	<		83	S		106	j
61	=		84	T		107	k
62	>		85	U		108	l
63	?		86	V		109	m
64	@		87	W		110	n
65	A		88	X		111	o
66	B		89	Y		112	p
67	C		90	Z		113	q
68	D		91	[		114	r
69	E		92	/		115	s
70	F		93	]		116	t
71	G		94	^		117	u
72	H		95	_		118	v
73	I		96	£		119	w
74	J		97	A		120	x
75	K		98	B		121	y
76	L		99	C		122	z
77	M		100	D		123	{

124	|	146	(c)	169	POINT
125	}	147	(d)	170	SCREEN$
126	~	148	(e)	171	ATTR
127	©	149	(f)	172	AT
128		150	(g)	173	TAB
129	■	151	(h)	174	VAL$
130	■	152	(i)	175	CODE
131	▬	153	(j)	176	VAL
132	■	154	(k)	177	LEN
133	▮	155	(l)	178	SIN
134	◣	156	(m)	179	COS
135	◥	157	(n)	180	TAN
136	■	158	(o)	181	ASN
137	◢	159	(p)	182	ACS
138	▌	160	(q)	183	ATN
139	◤	161	(r)	184	LN
140	▬	162	(s)	185	EXP
141	◢	163	(t)	186	INT
142	◣	164	(u)	187	SOR
143	■	165	RND	188	SGN
144	(a)	166	INKEY$	189	ABS
145	(b)	167	PI	190	PEEK
		168	FN	191	IN

192	USR	215	BEEP	238	INPUT
193	STR$	216	CIRCLE	239	LOAD
194	CHR$	217	INK	240	LIST
195	NOT	218	PAPER	241	LET
196	BIN	219	FLASH	242	PAUSE
197	OR	220	BRIGHT	243	NEXT
198	AND	221	INVERSE	244	POKE
199	<=	222	OVER	245	PRINT
200	>=	223	OUT	246	PLOT
201	<>	224	LPRINT	247	RUN
202	LINE	225	LLIST	248	SAVE
203	THEN	226	STOP	249	RANDOMIZE
204	TO	227	READ	250	IF
205	STEP	228	DATA	251	CLS
206	DEF FN	229	RESTORE	252	DRAW
207	CAT	230	NEW	253	CLEAR
208	FORMAT	231	BORDER	254	RETURN
209	MOVE	232	CONTINUE	255	COPY
210	ERASE	233	DIM		
211	OPEN #	234	REM		
212	CLOSE #	235	FOR		
213	MERGE	236	GO TO		
214	VERIFY	237	GO SUB		

ACERCA DEL AUTOR

Gary Plowman es Desarrollador de Juegos, Diseñador y Empresario de Internet de Dublín, Irlanda.

Fundó Gazzapper Games en 2014 y sus juegos tienen más de un millón de descargas hasta la fecha, incluyendo miles de descargas diarias.

Texto de la portada

Utiliza un Speccy, un emulador o una aplicación

El ZX Spectrum fue enormemente popular en la década de 1980 y fue responsable del boom de la primera etapa de la microcomputación en Gran Bretaña y Europa. Una nueva versión con Bluetooth está disponible ahora con Sinclair BASIC para iOS y Android.

Conoce cómo tantos programadores de dormitorios llegaron a programar con tan poco esfuerzo.

A continuación se muestra el código "Hello World" en BASIC.

Programa juegos de Arcade y Puzzle por diversión

www.ingramcontent.com/pod-product-compliance
Lightning Source LLC
Chambersburg PA
CBHW080426060326
40689CB00019B/4402